Black Diamonds

and other stories

Edited by Julia T. Lye

DeeBee

BLACK DIAMONDS AND OTHER STORIES
Copyright © 2021 by DeeBee Books

For information contact :
David Allan Hamilton:
davidallanhamilton00@gmail.com

ISBN: 9781896794495

First Edition: July 2021

10 9 8 7 6 5 4 3 2 1

Contents

BLACK DIAMONDS

Caz Little

THE TOWN REFERS TO IT AS THE TOWER. A CRUDE headframe of steel hastily bent, welded, and riveted onto the hilltop above Darnton. Towering into the air, its chaotic construction resembles a skeletal hand erupting from a grave. Twisted metal fingers outstretched towards the sooty town below and through its welded joints, the dim glow of electric shines, casting twisted shadows across the landscape. It is in these shadows that men begin to stir.

They wake in the dead of night, rising from their beds, leaving behind sleeping wives and children. Taking the breakfast lovingly made and left by the door the evening before. Hot potatoes placed into the front pockets of worn, waxed jackets. Warming hearts on the cold walk to the Tower. The men slip and skid in their sleepy dance across frozen cobblestones into the fields. Dew dampening hems of dotingly mended trousers. Boots turning from tan to dark brown. They travel easily in the darkness. Each man's path etched into his memory, through frosted blades to the gates of the Tower. Their feet lead them there every night.

A chain of children follow in their wake. Arms linked, they trace their own path like many nights before. Their yawns pulled away by the night breeze; noses and cheeks flushed. Only the grazing Galloways acknowledge them and lift their long heads as they pass, blind eyes gazing in their direction.

At the head of the chain walked Thud. Behind him, Rabbit and Sweep, followed by the Musgrave Twins and then Kit. Today was Kit's graduation into the Shallow Tunnels. Being the shortest of his age group he had been singled out as a Trapper Boy at age nine. Although he despised his time in the role, Kit had been diligent and serious about the job. Then a sudden growth spurt over the Autumn left him too big to fit into the tiny space by the trapdoor and he would be moved into the Shallow Tunnels with the older children.

At the end of many shifts, Kit would listen with green envy to the others talk about their time in the surface passages. Rabbit and Thud, the oldest of the group, had an ongoing tally of most carts delivered in a night. Their arguments over who pushed and who pulled often ended in fisticuffs, though Thud had always been told not to hit girls, he'd determined that Rabbit didn't count. Especially since he usually ended up with the bruises.

With their own carts to transport were the twins. At fourteen years old, they were content as long as they were together. On the long walks home, they repeated songs they had composed to make the time at work pass quicker. An animated Sweep filled any moment of silence with elaborate stories, in which he found dazzling jewels among the coals, leapt onto his faithful steed Dotty and delivered them to a far-off princess beyond the border of the town.

Dotty was in fact on the small side for a pit pony and only came up to Sweep's waist. One of the few Galloways whose sight hadn't been fully taken by the darkness. She was a sturdy little thing, afflicted by mange. Regardless of appearance, Sweep cared for her with a fierce intensity, and should any child dare question her bravery, he would scare them with tales of unknown horrors that lurked deep down in the blackness of the mine. Horrors that came to the surface when the Moonlight children slept in their beds.

Kit knew Sweep's stories weren't true, or at least were highly exaggerated, but it didn't stop the jealousy bubbling up inside him at the thought of them all together. In stark comparison to the other children, Kit's job had been to sit in solitude, opening and closing a small wooden door night after night, a canary his only companion. He would actually miss the bird and had been grateful for its company. Though he could never make it out in the darkness, he would occasionally take a couple of seeds from his pocket - previously smuggled from the garden bird table - fumble for the bars of its cage and wait to feel the little pecks of a beak on his fingers.

Even though he was a child of Moonlight, Kit had never adjusted to the dark of the Trapper hole. He had often tried and failed to explain it to the other children. It was much darker than in the Shallow Tunnels, where strings of electric hung across the low ceilings. Darker even, he dared to think, than the Deep Tunnels, where the men had beams of electric attached to their heads. At the mere suggestion of this, Thud would call "bollocks" and declare Trapper Boy a "Billy no mates." But Kit told the truth about the darkness. It erased everything it touched and all that remained was blackness.

He sat, sometimes up to 12 hours a night, swallowed by the dark. Periodically opening the door, fresh air blasting past him. Horror stories travelled by word of mouth about Trapper children hearing monsters in the dark and seeing ghosts. Kit had not met any ghosts, but there were nights when the rats would steal his bread and cheese, leaving him hungry.

The darkness played tricks on the minds of children. Some were so afraid, they had to be dragged back to the Tower at night and chained to their posts to stop them from fleeing. It was for their own good, Kit told himself. Better that, than end up like Little Moe. The men gossiped and speculated about her disappearance two winters ago. She must have been spooked and tried to find her way back to the surface, but they never found her, she's still down there somewhere, lost in the labyrinth of passages. Sometimes Kit liked to daydream she had found a way out, by some unknown exit and had run away to a distant place. Maybe she was a Sunshine child now. He knew deep down it wasn't true. Sweep once said she'd been eaten by the monster of the Pit, but unlike Sweep, Kit knew there were far worse things than monsters deep down in the mines.

II

AS THEY REACHED THE BASE OF THE HILL, KIT LET OUT A little sigh, his breath hovering in the night air. From now on, he would be in company every day. He had the other children now to talk to, to play with and to sing songs with. He closed his eyes and imagined the Shallow Tunnels harmonising together under the soft glow of electric.

Something small squeezed his hand then, and guilt shot

through him like a lightning bolt. Kit looked down at Boy Blue. He was a tiny mite, a Sunshine child, not accustomed to the night hours. He was holding Kit's middle fingers with that powerful grasp that only the smallest kids seem to have. He sucked the sleeve of his tatty, blue jumper, wet and frayed down to the cuff.

Kit had felt a responsibility for his replacement. Sunshine Kids knew nothing of the darkness of the Tower, or really any darkness at all. They slept through all their nights and spent their days in the bustling High Part of the town. The Tower's shadow barely darkened their doorsteps.

It wasn't the first time a Sunshine family had fallen on hard times. Usually, the Fathers or older sons would be offered up as labour to the Tower, but Boy Blue was the only remaining child of a single mother and there was need for a new Trapper Boy. Kit offered to collect the new recruit on the way to the hilltop that night. He had planned to share his knowledge and mastery of the door. How to time the air flow and notice the first signs of chokedamp. He would tell him how to keep his mind occupied and give him some seed for the bird. Most importantly, he needed to know the consequences that awaited if he wasn't hard-working.

Upon seeing the boy, he had instantly regretted the offer. The distressed Mother stood in the doorway, trying again and again to pull the wailing child from her skirts. Kit had been young when he started, but Boy Blue looked barely six years and his heart couldn't help but sink.

Kit walked as slowly as the line would allow, as Boy Blue trundled up the grass slope next to him. His little hand, surprisingly hot and clammy around Kit's. His eyes, the corners still crusted with sleep, wide and staring. As the peak of the Tower poked up above the horizon, he let out a gasp and launched himself into Kit's side. Winded, Kit stumbled to a halt, breaking the chain. A disgruntled Thud turned.

"What's the holdup?"

Rabbit looked down the line of heads and saw Kit and the Sunshine boy stopped in an awkward embrace.

"You better be faster than this in the tunnels, Kit," she hissed. "Or you can crawl back down your hole and take him with you."

Kit nodded, not wanting to anger his future friends before the night had even begun. He plucked one of Blue's arms from his waist, which only prompted a howl from the boy. The other children turned to shush the pair and continued their path to the hilltop. For a brief moment, Kit considered pushing Blue away and leaving him there on the hillside. His fate would likely be better than what was waiting for him in the Tower. Instead, he pulled the now whimpering child up into his arms and hurried to catch up with the chain.

III

KIT STOOD AT THE GATES AWAITING THE CHILDREN'S roll call. Across from the entrance of the Shallow Tunnels, the men were preparing to descend into the mine. He recognised each face, though most wouldn't know his. They distributed equipment amongst themselves, moonlight glinting off pickaxes, shovels, and chisels. A low hum of conversation peppered with dry coughs and smoke hung in the air as they took final drags of cigarettes. The old Trapper Boy studied the figures and wondered when his legs would start to bend that way.

A well-dressed man flitted about the crowd. The

Foreman reminded Kit of a moth in a top hat. His presence an irritant to the men he tirelessly hovered around, drab frock coat flapping behind him. Juggling a clipboard and electric, he quipped at the odd untied boot and askew hat. When he was done fussing, he carried himself over to the opening of the Shaft and began calling out names. Each man stepped forward and received a sharp rap on the head with the Foreman's cane. Testing the hat, the Foreman called it.

"You don't want to find out you've a faulty hat when the tunnel caves in on you, do you now?"

Kit knew the hat test well. It rattled his brain and made his ears ring, but he accepted the necessary examination and never once complained, the past casualties he witnessed being dragged from the tunnels ever present in his mind. The boy's arms and legs were covered in scrapes and grazes from squeezing himself into the Trapper hole night after night. Thanks to the hat, his head was the only place that didn't bear scars or fresh scabs. At the end of a long shift, he relished taking off that sweaty helmet and dragging his fingers through his flattened hair, causing his follicles to ache.

The name Brown was called and the air at the gates shifted. Brown, the man, was chewing the last bites of a jacket potato, steam still rising from its flesh. He was short and sinewy and held a reputation far greater than his stature, he was a Getter of fierce repute. No coal face could withstand the swing of his pick and no Government man the knuckles of his fist. Sweep said he single handedly took out 20 Candymen during the strikes. Tensions were always high between the men and the Colliery owners and the last time the Foreman had tried to hat check Brown, he ended up with a hole punched through his own grey top hat. On this night, he stared intently at his clipboard as Brown went past, to audible chuckles from the men.

Kit tried to keep well away from adult disagreements at work, worried he would be crushed by brawling men in steel toe boots. He gained his cautious nature from his Grandad. They used to walk across the fields together and wait by the Shaft, running through their own health and safety checks. And when Kit had lost count of the hours down in the darkness, it was the light from his Grandad's electric that he anxiously awaited.

At home, Grandad would insist on practicing maths and spelling before bed, to check all the smarts hadn't been knocked out of his grandson in the tunnel. Kit missed those conversations the most. His Grandad had been an intelligent man, full of knowledge and stories of the world. Anytime he wasn't down the pit he would be sketching. Kit watched in fascination as a blank page became filled with beautiful renderings in charcoal. A mother and child, the moon over the hilltops, distant fairytale lands of water and trees. After the accident, Kit snuck into his Grandfather's room to peek at his private sketchbooks, but in them he found frightening, twisted images of never-ending tunnels and crooked, tortured figures with shovels. He never looked again.

IV

THERE WAS A FLASH OF NAVY FROM ACROSS THE ROOM and there stood Boy Blue, his sleeve wedged firmly back into his mouth. He tugged on The Foreman's coat hem, who in turn examined the child over his clipboard. Kit couldn't make out his expression, but he seemed hesitant. Yes, thought Kit. This is a mistake, you know it's a mistake. He wouldn't let this kid into the mines. His clothes were clean.

His skin unblemished and so fair. He looked so delicate and so wrong against the shades of ash and grime of the men. They will have to find an older child, a Moonlight child.

But the Foreman made no move to dismiss the boy. Instead, he retrieved a small orange helmet, all too familiar to Kit, and placed it on the lads' head. It was comically large on Blue and fell down past his eyes. A tiny hand lifted up the brim for watery eyes to stare out. Now visibly upset and confused and finding no comfort from the men around him, Boy Blue started looking around helplessly. Both hands holding up his helmet, tears beginning to flow, he searched desperately for someone to save him. Small, panicked breaths left his mouth like a tiny steam train chimney. Just before Blue turned in his direction, Kit ducked down behind an empty cart. Shame submerged him. It's not my responsibility. He felt for the icicle of guilt in his heart that had been growing there since he first knocked on the Sunshine child's door. I've waited so long for this. He tried to reassure himself. It's not my fault.

A stern voice snapped him out of his spiral.

"Old Trapper Boy?"

It muttered to itself.

"What the hell is it called…"

Then footsteps.

"Ah," a face appeared over the cart, moustached lip curled. "There you are."

Kit was unsure if this was a statement or a question, but he leapt to attention with a little too much enthusiasm for 3am.

"Here, Sir!"

The volume prompted disgruntled looks from both the Foreman and Kit's new teammates. He even felt the eyes of the men from across the room. That meant Blue would be looking, too.

Thud spat on the floor.

The Foreman sighed and began allocating equipment.

"Right," he said, shoving a rope into Kit's arms, "you start as Hurrier today, you'll be teaming with Sweeney."

Sweep, who had spent that last while looking around the entrance for Dotty, spun round in horror.

"Oh, Sir!"

"Pipe down, Sweeney. You're not Driving today, Taylor needs a partner. Teach him the ropes, try to keep him alive, good lad."

Sweep, still aghast, turned his head towards Kit with such a look of disdain you would think Kit had turned Dotty into glue. His new partner offered up a small smile, to which Sweep scoffed and kicked loose grit at him.

Kit swallowed. A Hurrier it is. He'd often watched the children in the Shallow Tunnels when he was waiting for the lift to start up. The Hurriers tied ropes about their waists and pulled the carts through the passage, while the Thrusters pushed from behind. He could do it; he was certain. He'd studied the two usual teams, Rabbit and Thud and the twins, straining to get the carts up to the entrance, pushing with their hands and even their heads when the load was extra heavy. Sweep said sometimes the load weighed as much as a Shire horse.

"Bowes and Longstaff you're on tunnel A. Musgraves on B and Sweeney and the new one, tunnel C."

The Foreman shooed him toward the rest of the group who had begun the short walk down to the carts. Kit could see the faint glow of electric in the distance and his guilt was replaced with excitement. The passage was already brighter than he was used to from the full light of the moon unobstructed by clouds. He could even walk almost upright as he went down the gentle incline. Up ahead, Thud had reached the punchline of some dirty joke and Rabbit's cackle echoed back towards him. The twins' heads bobbed up and down in front of him, their feverish energy contagious as they started up a ditty. Even Sweep's mood softened at the sound of their tune and he began to hum along.

This was the beginning of a new life for the old Trapper Boy. He watched his new friends and basked in their presence. He would win their favour with his hard work, even Thud would be impressed. And then he could tell Sweep stories, he would sing along with the twins and show Rabbit his drawings. Kit could pinch himself. His Grandfather would be happy. He had finally got out of the hole.

Back at the entrance an almighty clang rang out. The ground beneath Kit's feet rumbled, sending pebbles skittering about. Then the whirring of heavy machinery started up and the familiar clunk, clunk, clunk, of the lift descending down the Shaft echoed throughout the Tower. Curiosity took hold of his head and he turned to look back towards the entrance. Eighteen men stood, stone faced and silent, crammed onto the lowering platform. At the front, barely reaching their knees was the figure of a tiny child. If Boy Blue was afraid, Kit couldn't see it. If he was crying, he couldn't hear. The little orange hat disappeared down into the dark.

AM I ONLY DREAMING?

Bonita Thatcher

SIX MONTHS AGO, I HAD A DREAM. THAT'S WHAT MY psychologist, Dr. Grayson, tells me anyway. I tell myself it was a dream, but it was so real to me, the man standing at the end of my bed. He was dressed in black trousers, a white shirt and had a silver-buckled belt at his waist. His jet-black hair slicked back, a scar on his left cheek. Stale cigarette smoke drifted in the air long after I had woken. His face was not friendly. I did not know him. And no, I hadn't been watching Al Pacino movies. My little world was in shambles. I had panic attacks, I jumped at my own shadow, and the circles around my eyes were becoming blacker and deeper. Tonight was the first time I was going to be alone overnight since what my family affectionately termed the 'incident'.

The giggles of excited children filtered in from the street. I watched them through the slats of the wooden blinds from the bedroom window. Their black capes were flying as they ran from house to house in search of treats. Pumpkin shaped buckets glowed in the low light. I wondered if he was out there now, watching me. I was glad I had put the sign on the front gate, No trick or treat here, Thank you. I just wanted to get through the night without any disturbance.

John was away on business. I had begged him not to go. My sister, who stayed with me when John was away, was on holiday. I think they thought they were doing me a favour, helping me deal with my 'situation'. What they didn't know is that I had seen him again. At the shopping centre on the downward escalator as I was going up. He was watching me as I got in my car at the train station. Dressed in the same clothes, a lit cigarette dangling from his mouth.

"I am not crazy!"

The noise outside began to grate on my tired brain. I rechecked all the doors to make sure they were locked and made my way to the living room at the back of the house. Shiraz in hand, I eased myself onto the brown leather, slowly releasing my legs in front me. I turned on Netflix and pulled my laptop onto my knees. Marking student reports could be a welcome distraction.

My phone lit up with a text from John. *Have a nice warm bath before bed. It will help you relax. Love you.* It was another diversion from the sleep I so desperately needed, and I took it. I found some vanilla scented tea light candles and bubble bath and turned on the taps.

The warm water engulfed my body as I sank into the claw foot bath. My toes surfaced and tickled the bubbles. I closed my eyes and attempted the meditation techniques I had been working on with the psychologist. I was in there for around five minutes before the silence and stillness began to irritate me. I felt vulnerable, lying naked in the bath. I got out and dressed in my pyjamas and reached for the sleeping pills in the bathroom drawer. They were for emergencies. I gulped them down with a mouthful of Shiraz and lay on the couch, cocooned in the multicoloured crochet blanket nan had made for me. She would have believed me.

I woke to canned laughter from some American sitcom and my drowsy eyes trying to adjust to the light from the silver lamp in the corner. I was warm and cozy. I had no idea of the time, but it was quiet. My fluffy, pink bed socks slid across the floorboards as I shuffled my way down the hall to my bedroom. I left the bedside lamp on, drew back the covers and lay my weary body on the electric blanket heated sheets. Then, the lights went out.

The house plunged into total darkness. I fumbled for my phone on the bedside table, but it was not there. My foggy mind raced as I tried to figure out what was going on. A fault in the lines I told myself. I slipped out of bed on John's side and searched for a torch in the drawer. I couldn't find one. My legs could barely carry me to the window. I looked out to see if any of the other houses had lights. The small, solar-powered lights gave a faint glow to the front garden. He was there, a shot of light reflected off his silver buckle as he moved. His body silhouetted against the white picket fence. I screamed, but the noise jammed in my swollen throat. I ran toward the kitchen. I didn't make it. I slipped in the hallway and heard a crunch in my foot on the way down. My right ankle radiated pain immediately, the throbbing unable to keep pace with my raging heart.

I dragged myself hobbling to the kitchen bench. My phone was not there. I searched the kitchen cupboard for a torch and was relieved to find one that worked. My focus turned to the rattle of the back door handle. The giant carving knife that I pulled from the wooden block felt cold and heavy in my shaking hands. I crouched down behind the island bench. I knew it was no good. I couldn't run, and I could only hide for so long. What did the psychologist keep telling me? Take control of your emotions, breathe, distract yourself. I sucked in a deep breath and screamed. The sound emanating from my body was unrecognisable.

I was momentarily distracted by a small flash of light on the chocolate rug near the couch. It was my phone. I dragged myself commando style across the floor. Someone was now at the front door, and I could hear knocking.

"Sarah, it's Eddie from next door, are you ok?"

"Enough," I breathed.

The lights came on, and I picked my sorry self off the floor. I began to limp to the front door, laying the knife on the bench as I passed. The porch light had come on, and I recognised Eddie through the frosted glass in the door. I unbolted the deadlock and turned the gold handle.

Eddie greeted me, dressed in a cowboy outfit, complete with hat, fringed waistcoat and a belt with a silver buckle. 'I jumped the fence and tried the back door, too. Hope I didn't scare you."

"Hello, yes, sorry, I'm fine. Tripped and sprained my ankle that's all."

"Do you need to see a doctor? I can drive you."

"I'm fine, it's just a sprain, I'll ice it and strap it."

"Are you sure Sarah? Are you here by yourself? Maybe you would like to come to ours for a bit?"

"Thanks for the offer, Eddie, I'll be fine."

"Call us if you need us."

I closed the door and made my way to the freezer, using the walls for support. Grabbing an icepack, I sat on the recliner, elevated my legs, and returned to the warmth of the blanket. I flipped open my laptop and searched for the emails from Dr. Grayson. I clicked on the one titled *Ways to stop anxiety attacks.* 1. Understand the anatomy of an anxiety attack; 2. Stop scaring yourself, 3. Calm yourself down, 4. Relaxed diaphragmatic breathing...

My phone lit up with a missed phone call message alert. I ignored it. The sleeping pills were retaking hold. Good. I needed to sleep. The unknown caller left a message.

"Sleep tight, Sarah. That blanket looks so warm." The crackling burn of a drawing cigarette and release of air was heard before the male voice said, "Sweet dreams."

EGO THE APPETITE

Patrick Fell

MY FIST CLEAVED THE AIR, TOUCHING NOTHING.

"You're useless, Ego," my opponent taunted me with a sneer.

Despa, the strongest person in my group and the academy's most promising new student, was my opponent today. He was the very embodiment of an Operator. Every jab I threw in his direction was anticipated before I even started, and every kick was nimbly sidestepped with a mocking grin. I fed more power to my Engine, a cobalt blue chain wrapped around my neck. Lightning crackled down my arms and legs, and I felt a renewed strength flood my limbs.

A desperate need to win this bout drove me to attack him in a frenzy. I had failed against my fellow students too many times, disappointed too many masters. They were trying to remake me in their image, but I wasn't like them. I was a good person, what they were trying to teach me went against my very nature. The problem was, I could not afford to fail anymore. If I didn't start showing progress soon, they would simply stop expecting anything more from me. Once they decided I was incapable of living up to my potential, my corpse would be their consolation prize.

Our current master, Operator Gravos, watched from the corner of the sparring room. His attention was mainly focused on Despa, but every now and then I could feel his gaze land on me from behind his red crystal Engine glasses. I wasn't sure what the glasses did exactly, but it had something to do with detecting soul energy and Glit, the dust-like substance that enables the creation of Engines. His dissatisfaction at the amount of power I fed into the Engine was obvious. As long as I could keep my soul energy flowing into the Charged Chain Engine wrapped around my neck, I was twice as strong and fast as a normal human. If I had better control over my soul energy, I could reach strengths and speeds rivaled only by the Gods. Unfortunately, I could only direct the barest trickle of power, so any Engine I used was just as weak as I was. Gravos could see how useless I was on every level.

I launched a flurry of punches at Despa, forcing him to use his weapon to defend against me. He wielded an Iron Staff Engine. A solid metal quarterstaff capped at either end by an auger. Feeding it soul energy enhanced the Iron Staff's durability and spun the augers at speeds capable of drilling through solid stone. It was a common Engine, and quite deadly in skilled hands. Despa flicked his Iron Staff left and right to knock my punches away, throwing me off balance. He didn't even bother to activate it with soul energy.

Frustration at my own weakness welled up inside me, cutting off my flow to the Charged Chain. Within seconds, my Engine sputtered, then died. With it went my enhanced strength and speed as the magically charged lightning vanished from my limbs.

"Give up, Ego," Despa spat at me, "You are no Operator. You're a disgrace; you can barely feel the touch of your Soul. Not like I can." His disdainful sneer punctuated his words.

I knew he had at least four different openings to finish the practice bout as the victor. He liked the attention toying with me gave him, it made him feel superior. The more superior he felt, the more anger and disdain he had towards his fellow trainees who wasted his time. And that was what being an Operator was all about. Strong negative emotions fed an Operators connection to his soul, making him powerful. Despa embraced these negative emotions even before he started training, the perfect Operator some would say. Our master looked at him in approval as our bout continued.

I may have had a high concentration of Glit in my body, but I couldn't touch it with my soul. I couldn't feel anger like the other trainees. When I was wronged, I showed compassion. When I was told I should feel hate, I felt regret. Despa was right.

I was no Operator.

I learned this horrible truth three months ago when I first arrived, and every day since, I sank further and further into despair. A successful Operator, the so-called heroes of our world, were at best vicious thugs and at worst insane forces of nature. The constant reliance on hate and fear to fuel their powers twisted their minds over time until they were no better than the monsters they hunted. The unsuccessful Operators however, the ones who didn't receive the Masters' stamp of approval, had it much worse. If a student failed to meet the expectations, they were killed and their bodies processed to extract the Glit in order to create new Engines. It was a no-win situation for me. Either I became a monster, or Gravos killed me for my Glit. Judging from my performance to date, I was fairly sure it would be the latter.

A sharp pain in my gut wrenched my attention away from my worries and back to the fight. Despa jabbed the end of his Iron Staff into my midsection, causing me to stagger several steps backwards while I struggled to remember how to breathe. Despa shook his head in disgust then looked to our Master. There was an unspoken question in his eyes which Gravos could see just as clearly as I did.

A quick nod from our Master was all it took. Despa turned his gaze back to me and a cruel smile stretched his face. My stomach sank. I knew what was about to happen even before he activated his Iron Staff Engine. The augers at either end begin whirring, yellow sparks spitting into the air from the sheer force they generated as they spun in place. A single touch from them now would pass through flesh and bone as easily as water.

Fear arrived, like a wave of acid through my chest. My connection to my soul was now much stronger than it had been a few moments ago, and my Charged Chain Engine came to life. I could suddenly feel my master begin to show an interest in me. Lightning crackled down my arms and legs, only this time the magical lightning also did something new. I could feel the electricity reach up through my spine to my skull, and time slowed down.

An image appeared before me, like ghosts acting out what was about to happen. I saw Despa clearly, he tired of the game and would finish it by thrusting the augers of his Engine into my head, killing me instantly but leaving my heart intact to harvest the Glit.

My fear surged at this revelation, causing my knees to tremble, and I suddenly heard Gravos's voice in my head.

"Your life ends tonight, one way or the other."

The bubble of acid fear causing my legs to tremble exploded inside me. I was not ready to die. Not here. The primal emotion surged through the connection to my soul like a rampaging bull, instantly causing it to expand from a single strand into a thick braid of power. My body practically moved of its own accord, and I slid to the side. Mere inches, but it was enough so that when Despa finally began his attack, his strike hit nothing. The auger whirred past my ear harmlessly, and a look of confusion crossed Despa's face. He hesitated, and his connection to his soul faltered. Those precious seconds stretched into long minutes thanks to my Engine, and my fear began whispering to me.

There was an initial urge to flee, to run and not look back, but I was cornered like a rat under the unforgiving gaze of Gravos. Unable to flee, the instinct to fight took over. It told me that this moment was a threat to my very existence and that threat had to be destroyed at all costs. The cold acid burn of fear was soon replaced by an intense heat. A burning star raged inside of me, and I was so consumed by it that not a single conscious thought could intrude.

Time snapped back around me, and I lunged towards Despa. My fist tore through the air with such speed that the air snapped in its wake like a miniature thunderclap. A snarl escaped from behind my clenched teeth, and Despa hastily raised his Engine in defense. There was an earth rendering crash as my fist hit the Iron Staff with such force that the

Engine shattered upon impact.

Shock registered on Despa's face as hot metal rained down around us in a deadly storm of shrapnel, but I didn't let up. The bones in my fist were broken after shattering the Engine, but I was incapable of feeling it under the burning rage of my soul. It screamed at me that my opponent was weakened under my onslaught and to strike again. I immediately slammed the palm of my other hand into his face, breaking his nose and showering us both in blood. This time, it was his turn to stagger, and then fall to his knees in defeat.

My burning soul was far from done.

In a blink, I found myself behind him with an arm wrapped around his neck, twisting with all my strength. Despa's eyes bulged as he clawed at my arms to get me to disengage. More blood flowed, this time my own from the gouges he tore into the flesh of my arm with his nails, but I felt no pain. His eyes twitched to Gravos, a cry for help within.

Our master did nothing but continue to watch with interest.

A loud snap echoed in the sparring room.

Despa's eyes went lifeless, and his tongue hung limply from his mouth. The burning emotion in my soul receded and I became aware of my loud breathing as the only sound in the chamber.

Realization quickly set in.

I had murdered a fellow student. Regret washed through me, dousing the burning flames and leaving only a cold emptiness inside. My connection to my soul dissipated like dust in the wind, and I collapsed next to the lifeless corpse that was once Despa.

Gravos approached me in silence and stood over me. I knew judgement would be swift and brutal. There was only one response to witnessing the weakest trainee kill the most promising future Operator of our group. I was numb inside after my unforgiveable sin, even if I wanted to fight my master in a futile attempt to save my life, I wasn't even able to feel a single wisp of my soul. I lowered my head and awaited the inevitable.

Instead of removing my head, however, he spoke.

"Well done, Operator."

I looked up at him in astonishment. His eyes crinkled in amusement behind the red crystal Engine lens, and he placed a hand on top of my head.

"You are confused, this is normal. We discussed how to break through your mental blocks preventing you from truly accessing your soul energy. We realized hate is not in your nature, but fear...ah that is a potent ally indeed and one you were raised to respect." He gave a negligent kick to the corpse at his feet. "Despa embraced the nature of an Operator, but he lacked your power. His sacrifice for your progress was an acceptable loss, he would have been a middling Operator at best despite his natural talents during his first few months here. Encouraging his hatred for you was easy, bringing out your fear was not."

My heartbeat pounded in my ears. I was going to live? I almost couldn't believe it. My voice eked its way out in a croak, and I asked the one coherent question my thoughts could form. "Why me?"

He laughed at my question, "Had you failed this test tonight, we would have at least created a powerful new Engine from your Glit. I am pleased you succeeded, however; a strong Operator is much more useful. Enjoy your victory, Operator Ego. You deserve it."

I was stunned. Emotions I couldn't explain warred within me. One part of me was sick and disgusted with Gravos and the other Masters, manipulating me into taking a life, but the other part that caused my heart to race in excitement was from my childhood dreams of adventure and power coming to life before me. It was... intoxicating.

While I wrestled with my thoughts, Gravos abruptly turned and walked towards the door of the sparring room, calling over his shoulder to me as he left. "Oh, and do be a dear and bring the body to the Mortician. He was expecting one body tonight, the fresher the better. Despa's Glit should make a fine new Engine for you."

The thought of receiving a new Engine sent a thrilling shudder down my spine, even though I knew what Gravos was doing. He was desensitizing me by having me haul the corpse of the man I just murdered down to the mortician. But it was a new Engine. One made specifically for me, not a common one given to trainees upon their arrival.

I was disgusted by Gravos and his attempts to corrupt me. If it were his body on the floor, I wouldn't have given it a second thought. Although, it's not like Despa was a good person, either. Had he killed me tonight and made an Engine from my Glit, he would have become a holy terror in his own right. You could say that by killing him, I saved countless others. I looked over his corpse once more, and I couldn't help but consider how much good I could spread across the land by using the Glit in his body rather than letting it go to waste.

It seemed perfectly reasonable to me once I began looking at it from a new perspective. I made up my mind and reached for his body, but I had completely forgotten about my broken hand. The sharp pain from the sudden movement caused me to swear and hiss in pain while cradling my injured hand to my chest.

Doing this one-handed would be a challenge. My gaze swept the sparring room for a way to transport the body when my eyes fell on the remains of his Iron Staff. It was incapable of being repaired, but perhaps I could harvest some Glit from the augers as they were still intact. I found a length of rope, and after fumbling one-handed for a while, fashioned a harness that I could use to lash the corpse to my back. As for the augers, I simply shoved them into Despa's clothes so they wouldn't fall.

His body still took more effort to haul to the mortician than I thought it would. I did manage to send a whisper of soul energy to my Charged Chain, but I was exhausted and drained so the extra strength it provided was almost no help at all.

"Ah, Ego." The mortician greeted me with a creepy smirk on his weathered face. "I guess that means I lose a hundred gold to Gravos. Unfortunate. I was rather looking forward to seeing what Despa would make from your Glit. No matter, no matter. Place it on the table." He brushed a thin lock of white hair behind his ears and rubbed his liver-spotted hands together eagerly.

I never liked the mortician, but like all Masters here, he was a powerful Operator despite his advanced age. Showing deference and respect was simply good survival instinct as well as good manners.

"I'm afraid I don't believe I can get him up, Master." I told him, holding up my hand for him to see. "I'm afraid it's broken." The apologetic smile I forced onto my face was a little slow, but I hoped he would chalk it up to my obvious pain since my hand was already a dark shade of purple by this point.

His eyes narrowed at me under layers of wrinkles, "Did that sound like a request?"

A cold sweat ran down my spine, and I lowered my head in subservience. The fear I felt now was only a trickle compared to what I felt fighting against Despa, but it was enough to increase the flow of soul energy to my Engine. Using my one good hand, I managed to wrench the body off my back and up onto the table. It was easier than I expected.

"Aha, I see Gravos was correct about your fear." He chuckled. "Use it boy. Embrace it like a lover as it whispers terrors into your heart, and you will be a force to be reckoned with."

He turned away from me and began working on Despa's body. I was thankful he didn't see the shudder that went down my spine from his words. It terrified me.

Before three months ago, I would have done anything to be picked for training as an Operator. Whenever the Lord's storytellers visited our village, I was enraptured by their epic sagas of adventure. They recounted the tales of famous Operators as they delved into the deepest dungeons of the kingdom, retrieving riches to dwarf the coffers of the wealthiest nobles, and recovering ancient Engines capable of granting god-like powers. I looked forward to every word they poured into my ears, but it was nothing more than honeyed poison.

My parents always warned me to beware what I wished for, but my imagination was set on fire at every tale spun by these masters of enticement. When my sixteenth summer rolled around, I was first in line to be tested and after they announced that I had a strong presence of Glit in my body, I was ecstatic. The others my age looked at me in obvious jealousy, while the older villagers looked on stoically, never cracking a smile.

I didn't understand their detachment at the time. I was practically bouncing in excitement and yet even my parents kept their faces perfectly neutral until the day I left. As I rode away on my first horse ever and surrounded by the regal guards of the kingdom, I glanced back towards my parents one last time. The cheerful wave of farewell died mid motion as my gaze fell on my mother. Tears rolled freely down her cheeks, and her carefully maintained neutral expression couldn't hide the haunted look in her eyes any longer.

I understood her grief now. Even if I survived, the son she knew was heading towards his doom. The shudder that went down my spine at the mortician's words wasn't fear, it was the tantalizing thrill of excitement.

"I just had a wonderful idea," the mortician announced, favoring me with his all too creepy smile. "Come here, I will instruct you on how to prepare a body to extract the Glit."

I balked, "Uhm, that's really not necessary, Master."

"Nonsense, this is a valuable skill. Quickly now, approach," he told me, holding out a thin bloody blade for me to take. I did as instructed, silently and obediently, but inside I screamed in horror. Not only forced into murder, now on their word I had to desecrate a body. I took the blade and looked down at Despa's corpse, seeing the skin on his chest already peeled back and exposing the muscle beneath.

"Now then, I already skinned him so we can skip that part," the mortician said in my ear, his breath hot and smelling faintly of rot and spices. "We will start with removing the muscle, here, and here." He pointed with a finger, dragging a fingernail over the indicated sections. "Then we will use the forceps to break the rib cage and expose the heart. From there the real work begins."

Sweat beaded on my brow as my gorge rose, but I forced it down. If I ruined the Glit by throwing up inside the chest cavity, the mortician may just kill me for ruining a perfectly good potential Engine. I followed his instructions, step by step. It didn't take long, but it felt like hours before I had the heart exposed.

"Excellent, now this part requires a more delicate touch. Technically, we could have just extracted Glit using a Misericord Engine and stabbing it directly into the heart without the need to expose it first, but much Glit is wasted in that manner." He removed a contraption from a nearby shelf that was all needles and tubes attached to what appeared to be a heart-shaped ewer. "This vessel can extract and store every speck of Glit from the body until we are ready to use it, which won't be long in this case because you will be creating an Engine this very evening with it. I have a pile of specially prepared Engine components in the back, use your connection to your soul to find one that resonates with you while I finish here."

I nodded numbly and left to find the components, unsure how I would even touch my soul while inside my own heart I felt just as dead as Despa.

True to his word, in the back I found a veritable treasure of components. Hundreds of devices of every make imaginable hung on walls or rested on shelves. Weapons of all sizes on one side, armor of all shapes on the other, and seemingly ordinary artifacts of everyday life in between. On one table, there even rested a doll. It was well worn, most likely having spent many years in the loving grip of a child.

When I leaned forward to examine a strange discoloration on its dress, I quickly realized it was blood.

My lip curled in disgust. Operators were a disease, there was no doubt in my mind anymore at this point. Eventually, they would corrupt the world with their power, and I was well on my way to becoming one of them. My gut churned. How I loathed these obscene keepers of power, they all deserved to die. Every last one of them.

Unsurprisingly, the hate triggered my connection to my soul. Since I wasn't activating the Charged Chain around my neck at the time, the connection had nowhere to go but outwards. An invisible pulse radiated from me, washing over everything in my vicinity. As the pulse faded, I felt a pull. I followed the sensation to a table in the center of the room, and my hand was drawn towards a simple looking cane with a bone handle. I picked it up, feeling the heft and shape of it in my hands and found it felt comfortable. This must be what the mortician meant when he said find a component that resonated with my soul.

Unwilling to return to the mortician already, I decided to wander amongst the other potential engine components. Nothing else caught my attention, and my soul didn't seem to resonate with any other item. I sighed, deciding to return to the mortician before he came looking for me. As I turned to leave, I saw a room in the back I had previously missed. Curious, I entered it and found myself in what appeared to be the mortician's office. My gaze was drawn to an item on the desk, a thin pointed dagger with a hollow glass bulb on the pommel which gleamed in the candlelight. I picked it up and immediately felt this was not a simple component, but one that had power. This must be the Misericord Engine the mortician spoke of earlier, a device that could extract the Glit from an Operator simply from stabbing them in the heart.

That is when the idea that shaped my fate first occurred to me. I wondered, could I create a brand-new Engine that could incorporate an existing one? Intrigued with the notion, I pocketed the misericord and brought both items back to the mortician, not caring at this point if he discovered I was stealing from him and killed me.

"Ah, there you are. I'm just about... there. He had more Glit in him than I thought." The mortician said as I returned to witness the final moments of his grisly work. He plucked the needles from the shriveled gray lump that was once a heart, then handed me the heart-shaped ewer which emitted a soft golden glow from the Glit it contained. "Here is your reward, boy. Take it and insert the needles into your body, an artery is best but anywhere blood flows freely will do. Then grip your component tightly and focus on what you wish it to do, but I recommend keeping it simple. Your thoughts can influence the kind of power the Engine will produce, but many an Operator ended up with practically useless Engines because the ideas they had were too complicated. That is why most Operators will create common, well established Engines for their first attempts. I remember one idiot in particular tried to infuse his Engine with the power of immortality. He succeeded, but only for as long as he could keep the Engine powered from his connection to his soul. Soon as the connection died, so did he." He let out a malicious cackle. "It was educational and amusing."

I struggled to keep the grimace off my face, focusing instead on the questions I had instead of this creature's dark sense of humor. "I also retrieved the remains of Despa's Iron Staff Engine; I believe there is still some Glit present in them.

Can I use them to enhance the Engine I am about to create?"

"If it was still intact, yes. Unfortunately, since the Engine was damaged it will remember that damage and incorporate it into the new one. You would end up with just another broken Engine by the time you are done. I will take them and extract the Glit to be used with a new project." The mortician took the broken augers and began walking away with them. "Feel free to begin, I will return shortly."

Left to my own devices, I sat down on the floor and placed the cane across my thighs. My fear told me to play it safe, to use the lessons I learned to create a common Engine. But my recent experiences at the hands of the Masters were still fresh. Manipulating me into killing Despa, forcing me to dissect his corpse, even the doll with the blood stains. All of these memories were reminders that Operators were evil and needed to be destroyed. I firmed my resolve, my entire body tensing up with what I was about to attempt.

Retrieving the Misericord Engine from my pocket, I placed it on the floor next to me. Next, I took the heart ewer and cleaned off the needles as best I could before I inserted one into my left arm with a grunt, then for good measure, inserted another needle into my right arm. My preparations complete, I gripped the cane in my left hand, and the Misericord Engine in my right.

As the Glit from the heart ewer entered my bloodstream, I kept one thought firmly in mind. The power of the Glit built up inside my body and rushed down towards my hands, bathing the items I held with my intent. As the crescendo of power built, I whispered my intent out loud.

"I want to kill Operators."

That's what I said, but at the very last second a brief thought overrode my intention. It was the selfish child in me who still wanted to be an Operator, shouting his craving for power into my soul.

There was a blinding flash of light. When it cleared, I no longer held two items. Instead, I clutched a single Engine in my hands. It was still a cane for the most part, but it had some differences. The original bone handle had morphed into a hollow tube of bone, while the other end of the cane tapered to a needle thin point. It was so thin in fact, I worried it would bend or break at the slightest touch. Gingerly pressing it into the stone floor, I was surprised to see the tip pierce the stone and sink in as if the floor were as soft as clay.

I stood and examined my new Engine. It was beautiful.

"Already done, I see." The mortician said as he re-entered the room dusting his hands off. "Well, don't keep me in suspense boy. Tell me what you made."

My eyes locked onto his, "The Misericord Cane."

"The…" His eyes went wide. "Misericord? Boy, did you steal from me?"

His anger scared me, rightfully so. It deepened my link to my soul, but I needed more. I needed him to embrace his own soul, it would terrify me. Knowing it would anger him even more, I responded only with an arrogant nod.

He snarled an ugly sound. "You dare! Hand it over and I will consider killing you quickly for your audacity." He pulled the sleeve of his robes on his right arm up to his elbow, exposing a bracer on his arm which appeared to hold a variety of spikes. It was a Goring Band Engine, very rare, very powerful. The spikes began to whirl around the mortician's forearm, apparently eager to seek my flesh. "Otherwise," he continued. "I will pin you to the ground like an insect and extract your Glit while you still live."

His words pushed my fear to new heights. It was exactly what I needed.

My connection to my soul surged, and I fed that power directly into the Misericord Cane. It responded immediately by detaching the hollow bone tube from the rest of the Engine. A glowing green, translucent tube connected the detached pommel to the rest of the Engine. Before either of us could react, the lower half of the cane shot like an arrow directly towards the mortician's heart.

The mortician staggered back with a grunt as the needle tip pierced his chest and lodged into his heart. The bloodshot white of his eyes grew in alarm and he gripped the haft with both hands and attempted to pull it out. A blood curdling shriek escaped his lips as the cane fought to remain where it was.

I could not help but admire the old creature's fortitude. A lesser man would already be dead, and still he fought the Engine lodged in his chest. It was then that I saw the telltale golden glow of Glit begin to travel down the translucent green tube that connected the haft to the hollow bone pommel. My soul's link to the Misericord Cane screamed what to do, resisting its instructions never even occurred to me.

Placing the end of the bone tube in my mouth, the golden Glit reached my tongue. There was no taste, only the incredible sensation of the pure essence of life filling my soul to the brim. I swallowed reflexively as the Glit filled my mouth, and my soul exploded in ecstasy.

The mortician's screams ended as the last of the Glit was drained from his heart. The last of the golden dust streamed into my mouth and I swallowed it all, down to the last speck. I had never felt more alive than I did at that moment.

And I wanted more.

Over the next few weeks, I hunted down all my fellow students. At first, none of them even considered me a threat. No one connected the death of the mortician to the missing student. After all, it was impossible for Ego the weak to best one of the oldest and strongest Operators at the academy. At first, their faces held only contempt when I confronted them. Over time, the contempt changed to wariness, then eventually to outright fear. It was perfect. I drained every last one of them of Glit, and I couldn't stop. I wanted more. I needed more.

Eventually, Gravos caught up to me. Too many students had been found dead, Glit drained from their bodies. My old master was forced into action or the academy would collapse due to a lack of students. He tracked me down, discovering the cave I used as a haven in between hunting down the students. I returned from one of my hunts to find Gravos already waiting for me. By then, however, I was bursting at the seams with power, and a variety of Engines taken from my victims after they died.

He didn't lack power of his own, however. Armed to the teeth with a variety of Engines, he attacked me without a word as soon as I appeared. A Fisher Engine on his wrist launched a blackened fishhook at me where it lodged into my shoulder. It hurt, but the most dangerous part was when it began pulling back towards the bracelet he wore, throwing me off balance as I fought the constant drag. Within the same breath, he threw what appeared to be small bundles of dead vines at my feet. It became clear that they were Wicker Construct Engines when they each unfolded into puppets and began wrapping themselves around my feet in an attempt to trip me. Over his shoulder, I saw a shimmering red sword blade hovering in the air. A Dragon Tail Engine, a weapon capable of independently guarding any attack from the rear, as well as providing another method of offense. Spreading his hands, a whip of liquid fire came into being. I never even heard of an Engine like that before.

None of it did him any good. The Misericord Cane could not be defended against or avoided. No physical barrier could impede it, no power or energy could turn away its deadly tip. It pierced his heart despite all of his Engines, and the look of shock on his face as I began devouring his Glit was one I would cherish until my dying day, which, admittedly could have been a very, very long time.

After Gravos fell, I took his Engines as well. The most useful one to date, aside from my precious Misericord Cane of course, was the Red Crystal Engine he wore. As I suspected, it allowed me to see the Glit inside everything, people and Engines alike. With it, I hunted Operators across the world to consume, and I was so successful in tracking these creatures of evil that they soon fell into the realms of myth and legend, themselves.

I still needed to feed, however. I reasoned potential Operators could start the cycle of fear and hatred once more, so I began hunting them as well. A pleasant side effect of consuming Glit was that I no longer aged, so I could hunt these harbingers of doom until the end of time. I would protect the world from these monsters ever coming back.

Except... after feeding for hundreds of years it was getting harder and harder to find more sources on which to feed.

They tried to make me into a monster, but I defied them all. It started with dehumanizing me, calling me names like pathetic, or Ego the weak. Then they tried painting me as the monster, like one of them. Ego the Appetite. Disgusting. I'm the one who kills the monsters. I'm the one keeping the world safe. No one else.

ME.

And while the Glit inside you wouldn't qualify you to become an Operator, I am so very, very hungry. It's taken all of my willpower to hold off on feeding immediately to tell you my story. I know you're scared, but now you know why you have to die.

Shh-shh-sh. No crying. I'm a good person, really, I am. In fact, you could even call me a hero. Maybe even the greatest hero in history.

Close your eyes, this will only hurt for a few minutes.

SAMMY PETERS

Janet Edwards

IT WAS MAY, AND THE MAN ON THE TELEVISION WAS talking rain when I met Sammy Peters. It was nearing five p.m. on a typical rainy Tuesday when I had stopped by The Wellington pub before catching my train home. Sammy was at the bar, quietly drinking a pint while gazing happily around at his fellow patrons. I had not seen him in there before, though admittedly, the pub was not my local. The Wellington was known for its desolate atmosphere and penchant for a spontaneous brawl, which made the smile on Sammy's face so striking. I chose a spot at the bar, leaving one empty stool between me and Sammy, thinking that after a drink I would have the courage to say hello. But it was he who spoke first.

"Do you think it will ever stop?"

His voice was low and honeyed, and as I turned to face him, I felt a thrilling stir in the pit of my stomach. Those golden-brown eyes and sheepish smile that showed off one crooked tooth captivated me immediately.

"The rain," he continued, nodding his head to the tv behind the bar, "do you think it'll ever stop?"

I followed his gaze to the news reporter and mumbled something about it being North West England and when did it ever stop raining - but my mind was elsewhere. I wanted to know this man. For the next hour we talked with the candor of two people who had known each other for years. By the time he walked me to my train, we had made plans to see each other that coming weekend. And while my head was delirious with the anticipation of a potential new love, nothing could have prepared my heart for the tumultuousness of the next five months. I learned to love - to truly love another person. More significantly, I learned that even with the best of intentions, love is simply not enough. A harsh lesson indeed, but one I suppose I was meant to learn. I often think back to that Tuesday and wonder if I had just caught my train after my shift as usual, could my life have remained safe and uninterrupted? But life always has other plans for us, and whatever compelled me that day to stop in for a drink ended up giving me a profound experience I would not soon forget.

His birth name was Tom Hughes. Sammy was one of the three personalities that occupied a space in the bewildering mind of Tom. Perhaps because I met him first, it was Sammy I grew to love. He was soft-spoken, kind, and loved me with a passion I had never known before. I always wished I had had more time with Sammy. We seemed to only find a day here or there before the switch would occur and I would find myself with Tom or Brent. Tom, a decent but serious man, enjoyed my company well enough, though I believed he merely tolerated me for Sammy's sake. Brent, who was more cautious with his words, talked mostly of old cars or fiddled haphazardly with the model trains in his flat, more to just keep his hands busy it seemed. He spoke of his time in the war, though I could never pinpoint which one he believed he was in, so I wasn't certain of how old Brent thought himself to be. He reminded me very much of my father. The switch to Brent often took a day or two, and I became more aware of the signs when this was occurring. Sammy on the other hand, could arrive within hours of being around me, something I took as a testament of his genuine love for me. Whether that was true or not, I would never know.

It was not until late summer when I met the third alternate, a woman named Joan. Tom had told me there were three, but up to that point I had only known Sammy and Brent, and Tom wouldn't share much about the third. I came to understand why. Joan was the mother-figure, the matriarch of Tom's mind, and she was cruel. On this particular summer evening when Sammy and I were enjoying supper at my local pub, I instinctively brought my napkin to his face to wipe food off his chin, and he startled me by grabbing my wrist and slamming it down onto the table. In a rush of confusion, I looked at him and before I could speak, I saw his eyes had widened, the black of his pupils large and alarming. His forehead furrowed and he squeezed his eyes shut and relaxed his grip on me, but he did not let go.

"Don't," was all he said to me. And so, it began.

What surprised me the most was how fast Joan would appear, sometimes within only an hour, and other times like at the pub, mere moments.

Once, after Sammy and I had made love and were talking of plans for the evening, he grew unusually quiet as he lay still beside me. When I looked over, I saw his eyes had widened and I knew it was happening. But before I could get away, Joan pulled at my hair so suddenly and with such hatred that she ripped a small chunk of skin from my scalp.

Another time shortly thereafter, as I stood reapplying lipstick in the mirror at Sammy's bathroom sink, she hurled a book at me from the hallway, missing my head by mere inches and shattering the bathroom mirror. A week after that, she locked me in a bedroom closet for over thirty minutes after finding pictures of me in my bra on Sammy's phone.

By mid-August when I worked up the courage to speak to Tom of this, he was guarded and would not open up much to me. His despondency and lack of desire to speak of Joan was heartbreaking, but I longed to understand. Through a few brief conversations, Tom confided in me that Joan was his mother's name. He didn't tell me what became of her, but it was obvious to me that this was someone Tom had been fighting to keep at bay for years and was now failing. I began to wonder if my presence in his life had aggravated the Joan personality. Was it possible Tom had been doing well up to that point to keep her away? Was it my fault? Though the more pressing question on my mind was, what had she done to him?

The catalyst of it all came about on my birthday in late September. Sammy had painted for me a canvas of dark blue with a pale-yellow moon, with small specks of moonlight cascading down. I planned on hanging it over my bed so that every night when I lay down, I would imagine that Sammy and I were laying under the same moon. Sadly, and very suddenly, Joan destroyed it. She ripped it from my hands and cracked it against the corner of the dining room table, leaving a gaping hole in place of the beautifully painted moon. She called me a whore and told me I wasn't worthy of gifts. She said Sammy was not in his right mind when he painted it, that he was simple-minded and couldn't see who I really was. She seethed at me and vowed to warn Sammy of me. I left his flat in tears that night and did not visit again for nearly two weeks.

In the end, I spent most evenings with Brent, who looked uncomfortable and didn't have much to say to me. He would sit at the table and continue to nervously fidget with his trains. Tom, in a rare candid moment with me, told me his doctor was trying a new medication and that it was working to keep Joan away. In an ironic twist of fate, Sammy too, began to disappear.

I hung on as long as I could, but only saw Sammy briefly, maybe twice more. His eyes were sad when he looked at me, and I knew he would not be able to love me anymore. Not like before. I couldn't help but feel that Joan had won.

On my last evening with them, I broke down. Through my tears, I asked of Tom the very same question Sammy had asked me the day we met in the pub.

"Do you think it will ever stop?"

ALERT

Briana Dobson

FOUR YEARS AGO, MY DAD, EVERYONE'S FAVOURITE neighbour and cardiologist decided that my mom had ruined his life and that it was time she had her own heart broken. Dad quickly went from being a pillar of the community to the most hated man in the province, if not the country. I think a lot about what he put Mom through, and I am thinking about it as I stand in my bedroom staring at the top shelf of the bookcase he had built for me the Christmas before I turned five. Surprisingly, he had allowed me to take it to Mom's, but this was only just after they had separated. At that point, I do not think Dad's hatred for Mom had quite manifested as he still believed they would be together again.

My younger brother is in his own room rehearsing the speech he is going to give later today to thousands of people outside Parliament. At 13, he is becoming a well-known activist for missing children and an opponent of Crawford's Law, which was created seven years ago to ensure that Amber Alerts would no longer blast on cell phones disturbing the peace of Canadians between 8pm and 8am.

The law was named after Dennis Crawford, who angrily launched a social media campaign berating the government for sending out alerts regarding the whereabouts of other people's children he did not know from communities he had no ties to. He was successful, because the government in power decided that the public should not be inconvenienced by these alerts or be obligated to think about possible kidnappings during the evening when they are home with their own families. Besides, as Crawford had pointed out, the "alleged" missing children were not truly in danger as most of the Amber Alerts involved "parents just wanting to spend extra time with their children."

I am still staring at the bookcase when I notice that in between a long-forgotten copy of the Velveteen Rabbit and a book about puberty that I never actually read sits my hot pink sequin diary. Reaching up with my right hand, I pull it out from in between the books. I grasp my diary with both hands and blow five years of dust off the top spine. The padlock is long gone, courtesy of my nosy brother, but after opening the diary to its first page, I can see the ink remains:

April 11th

Dear Diary,

How are you? I am finally ten years old. I got you today for my birthday! My mom also got me a weird book about puberty and the yellow pea coat I wanted. I got to wear the coat today to school. James got me a silver sea horse necklace because those are my favourite animals. I will introduce myself to you. I am in grade four and I have one brother named Max. He is eight. I live with my mom, James, and my cat, Cheddar. My mom and James are going to get married next year, and I am going to be a junior bridesmaid. My dad is a doctor, and he fixes hearts. He lives with Angeline. I hope they get married so I can be a junior bridesmaid for them too. I like to figure skate and when I am 16, I am going to go to the Olympics. I'm sorry. I have to go now because me and Max are going out for dinner with my dad for my birthday and I have to get ready.

Sincerely,

Lucy Ferguson

P.S. I promise to write to you every day but not on Saturday because it's my birthday party.

If I could cry, this page of my diary would be soaked with tears. I know how I would like to remember Dad, but there are things about him I cannot forget. I remember almost everything about my tenth birthday and the things I was not there for in person, I learned about later from eavesdropping on Mom's adult conversations, when she was finally ready to talk about the day I turned ten.

* * *

APRIL 11TH IS BOTH MY BIRTHDAY AND PIZZA DAY AT school. That means that not only do we eat pizza for lunch, but also homemade cupcakes from Ms. Farrington-Fox. She is everyone's favourite teacher because she brings cupcakes for the entire class when one of us has a birthday.

After we finish eating, Ms. Farrington-Fox announces that it is time for Current Events. She explains that because we had to cut Language Arts short before lunch, we can continue colouring our Canada maps if we have not finished.

I pull out my map and a purple pencil crayon from inside my desk to continue colouring. I spread the sheet out in front of me, look at it and sigh. When I had started colouring the map, I had decided to press a thick line around the borders of the provinces and territories and then colour the land mass inside a shade lighter. My colouring method was going great until I realized that I had to colour all the small islands around Nunavut the same way and colouring all the islands had gotten boring fast.

"I don't know why you are spending so much time making it perfect. It's just getting thrown out at the end of the unit anyway," says one of the most annoying people ever.

I turn my head slowly to the left and Jake is raising his eyebrows up and down over and over at me. He has a stupid smile on his face. I roll my eyes at him and in response, he reaches over and plants his right thumb in the corner of my map leaving a greasy cupcake print in the middle of the Pacific Ocean.

"Jake!" I yell with exasperation.

Ms. Farrington-Fox demands for us to knock it off and I quickly shove my map back in my desk now that it is ruined. Last week, Ms. Farrington-Fox had reorganized the classroom so that we were sitting in rows of two. I wanted to sit next to Nuri, but Ms. Farrington-Fox sat Jake and I together. Sometimes I like Jake and other times I do not. He is loud and constantly jumps around like a demonic grasshopper both in the classroom and out in the yard. It is bad enough dealing with Jake at recess, but now I sit with him in class as well.

As soon as Ms. Farrington-Fox asks who wants to go

first for current events, unsurprisingly Jake jumps out of his seat and starts speaking.

"Okay, so we drove by Parliament on Saturday and there were like a billion people there yelling with signs. My mom said it was a riot, so we had to leave before they started breaking things and making fires."

Jake's clearly talking about the Crawford's Law/Amber Alert protest that had happened on the weekend. James and my mom already told me all about it because we had driven by too and I wanted to know why there were so many people around. My parents explained why people were angry but did not mention anything about the possibility of fires.

Before Ms. Farrington-Fox can say anything about Jake's current event, Nuri yells at him, "It wasn't a riot! It was a protest for Solange Singh and the Abadi twins!"

"Those kids that died?" Jake asks. He looks confused, but he always looks confused. Jake's in the lowest reading level group in the class. Ms. Farrington-Fox had told me that one of the reasons she moved me next to Jake is because I will be a good influence on him with reading.

Logan, who reads way better than Jake, but has no volume control, answers his question before Nuri can. "They were MURDERED stupid!" he screams.

Jake finally sits down looking a little sheepish. Jake may be loud and obnoxious, but he does not like being yelled at. Ms. Farrington-Fox chastises the entire class, explaining that if we cannot do Current Events without screaming at each other than we cannot do Current Events at all. There is immediately a sea of voices pleading to continue with Current Events.

We like that Ms. Farrington-Fox has Current Events hour every Wednesday because that is our time to talk about all the "scary" life things going on that the adults never want to talk to us about. Once Ms. Farrington-Fox is satisfied that we understand that screaming will not be tolerated, she explains to the entire class who Solange and the Abadi twins are and what the protest is about.

I am only half-listening to Ms. Farrington-Fox when I turn and look over at Jake who is uncharacteristically quiet as he stares down at his hands in his lap. I feel bad and ask him what is wrong.

Jake shrugs. "I don't know. I thought I had something smart to say. I just thought my parents were right about there being fires and I thought it would be cool to talk about because I think I am going to be a firefighter when I grow up."

I do not really know what to say, so I reply, "Oh," before adding, "it's okay to be wrong."

Jake mumbles thanks and then we listen to Aiko and Camille talk about their boring current events.

★ ★ ★

MAX IS NOW PRACTICING THE PART OF HIS SPEECH about Solange Singh and the Abadi twins. Max's research into the events surrounding the Singh and Abadi cases complements my memories quite well. I lay down on my bed and shut my eyes even though I am not tired. I am never tired. Sometimes it is just easier to remember things when you shut your eyes.

On the day of my tenth birthday, Crawford's Law had been in effect for 18 months. There had only been a handful of Amber Alerts issued during that time in all of Canada, but there were two cases, both from Ontario that caused public outrage, Solange Singh and the Abadi twins.

Right after Thanksgiving weekend, an Amber Alert was issued for Solange. She was 13 and had just immigrated to Toronto with her family from Guyana. I remember that Amber Alert well because the sound my mom's phone made caused her to jump and spill hot coffee on herself while Max and I ate our morning cereal. I had questioned if she was mad about the loud noise, but she said no, and that she hoped they found Solange soon. I started reading newspapers at that time and learned that Solange went missing the night before while walking home from a friend's house. Police concluded it was a stranger abduction and asked the public for information. They never did find out what happened to Solange. One of the major newspapers published a poll indicating that after the disappearance of Solange, 23% of Canadian's were in favour of abolishing Crawford's Law. I had to ask Mom and James to explain to me about polls and percentages.

The Abadi twins were also from Toronto and went missing three weeks before my birthday. They lived with their dad, but their mom wanted to keep them longer after Easter, so she just did. Shortly after the Amber Alert was broadcasted on a Tuesday morning, I heard Dennis Crawford being interviewed on the radio explaining that it was not really an abduction, but rather just a custody case and that the mother was probably trying to prevent her kids from being taken overseas by their father. A few days after he was interviewed on the radio, they found the Abadi twins and their mom in North Bay. I remember seeing photos of the 4-year-old boy/girl twins in the newspaper under the headline "Missing Twins Case Ends in Murder-Suicide." It turned out that their dad, Moe Abadi, was born in Canada and that it was their mom, Sarah Simpson, who was from another country. England, to be exact. To this day, I have no idea why Crawford would assume their dad was trying to take them to another country. I asked James if he knew, but all he said was that it was complicated, and we could talk when I was older. After that case, another poll was completed indicating that 38% of Canadian's thought Crawford's Law should be abolished. With math not being my strong suit, I had been excited to show Mom and James that I could identify changes in the poll percentage.

Of course, at 10-years-old, while I am waiting for my dad to pick me up, neither the missing and murdered kids nor the issues surrounding Crawford's Law are on my mind.

★ ★ ★

DAD ARRIVES AT EXACTLY 5:00PM TO PICK US UP. MAX and I are outside on the front porch waiting with James. James has just finished taking some birthday photos of me posing on the porch. Max managed to successfully dodge every photo James tried to take of him.

"Hey guys!" Dad cheerfully hollers from outside the front of his car on the side of the road. You can spot Dad's red car anywhere with its licence plate DR FERGS. I once heard Mom mention to James that he might as well get a license plate that reads NARCISSIST. Even though I do not know what the word means, it is a suggestion that I feel I should never mention to Dad.

Max runs up and gives Dad a hug and I hang back on the porch doing my best model pose so he notices my new coat.

"Happy Birthday, beautiful!" Dad bursts as he throws his

arms open wide. I run to give him a hug. I am happy he is in a good mood. "That's a great colour on you!" he grins. I notice that even though it is chilly out, Dad is not wearing a coat and he is sweating.

"Okay Mike, so 8pm?" James half-asks, half-directs from the porch.

Dad's grip on me tightens and he barks, "I know!" at James. Dad's unpleasantness towards James is normal, so I think nothing of it.

"Okay, yeah, well it's Lucy's birthday so just call me or Elena and let us know if anything changes..." James stumbles. He pauses, "Like if you are running late or something." James is forever trying to be nice to Dad even thought I do not think they will ever be friends. I honestly do not know why he bothers.

Dad ignores James and saunters to the driver's side of the car. James smiles and waves goodbye to us and we turn and get into the backseat of the car.

"Hey, where is Angeline?" I wonder. The front passenger seat is empty, and I am disappointed not to see Dad's girlfriend, who was the one who suggested a birthday dinner. I really like Angeline. She is fun and keeps Dad in a good mood. When Angeline is around, he does not usually talk about Mom.

"She got stuck at work," Dad says quietly. He turns around and smiles. "I guess that means you get the front seat, Birthday Girl!"

He does not have to tell me twice. Even though I am wearing a dress, I quickly hop over the centre console and climb into the front seat as my brother stakes claim that he gets the front seat on the way home even if it is my birthday.

★ ★ ★

I BOLT UPRIGHT ON MY BED WHEN I HEAR MOM YELLING to Max that they need to leave, or they will be late. Cheddar, who must have entered my room while I had my eyes closed, is hunkered down by the doorframe staring at me.

I place both feet on the ground and slowly stand up, not wanting to scare him. "Hey, Cheddar baby," I whisper as I take a step towards him. Even though I move slowly, he freaks out and takes off down the hallway making enough noise for ten cats.

Disappointed, but not surprised with Cheddar, I quickly leave my room, head downstairs, and follow Max outside. I wait with him on the front porch for Mom, who despite being ready to leave two minutes ago, is now inside looking for her glasses.

★ ★ ★

WITHIN FIVE MINUTES OF SITTING AT THE TABLE, A Shirley Temple with a yellow umbrella is placed in front of me by our server. Max has one with a blue umbrella. When Angeline had asked where I wanted to go for my birthday dinner, I said any restaurant where I could have a Shirley Temple. Angeline had promised Shirley Temples and she sure delivered.

"I had very strict instructions to bring you a Shirley Temple with a yellow umbrella," the server says cheerfully. I look for her nametag before responding.

"Thank you, Thea. Yellow is my favourite colour and it's my birthday," I beam.

"Oh, don't you worry, I was told that too when the

reservations were made… Lucy…" she responded with a wink. Of course, Angeline would have told her my name to make me feel even more special.

"I'm Max and my birthday is in two months," my brother, who does not want to feel left out pips up. Thea smiles and instructs Max that she expects to see him back for his birthday. She then tells us how much the colour of our blue eyes reminds her of her niece and nephew back in Sweden. Dad advises Thea that we got our eye colour from him. I think about adding that it is Mom who is half-Swedish and not Dad, but I do not want to risk upsetting him.

Dad, Max, and I have a great time talking about school and sports while I drink my Shirley Temple. Dad asks Max when he wants to start hockey and Max says never. He hates going to the arena to watch me skate because it is too cold. He says he is perfectly fine doing karate and soccer. After we place our food order, Dad tells us about a heart transplant he did on a baby the day before, which prompts Max to announce that, when he grows up, he will also be a doctor and they will do transplants together. Dad the sports fanatic may be disappointed that Max does not want to play hockey, but he is pleased that he wants to be a doctor like him.

"Will Angeline meet us later?" Max asks.

"No. She is out with friends," he mutters.

"But I thought she had to stay at work?" I question.

"She had to work and then go see friends. The point is that she isn't coming," Dad clarifies with a huff.

Max and I both take the hint that this is the end of the conversation regarding Angeline. For the next few minutes and until our food arrives, Dad is silent and busies himself texting on his phone. I do not ask who he is texting because most of the time it is just work stuff anyway. It is surprising how many people in Ottawa need their hearts fixed. Dad puts down his phone and picks up a napkin to wipe his glistening forehead. Just as I am about to question why he is still sweating and if he is sick, I am distracted by the arrival of our food.

Somehow, while stuffing our mouths with tacos, we got on the topic of what I got for my birthday. I tell Dad that Mom got me a diary and the yellow coat (I leave out the puberty book) and that Max got me a gift certificate for the Cineplex. I realize that I forgot to make note of that in my diary and will have to add that detail when I get home.

It is kind of an unspoken rule that Max and I do not mention James around Dad because sometimes just mentioning his name infuriates him. It is like Dad is reading my mind though because as I have an internal debate as to whether I mention the necklace, he points at my chest and asks, "Is that a real diamond?"

I feel my cheeks go red. I look down at my chest and pull up the sea horse charm to look at the 'diamond' in its eye. It is not actually a diamond. James had explained it was cubic zirconia, promising that when I am older, he will get me one with a real diamond in it since it is my birthstone.

"Oh, it's not real. It's just a fake diamond," I reassure Dad.

"Did you get that for your birthday? Was it from James?" he challenges.

I slowly nod in response to both questions.

Dad's face goes red and I can see him grind his teeth even though his mouth is shut. I look down at my plate of food. Out of the corner of my right eye, I can see that Max is doing the same.

"I see," Dad says. I look up and watch as he again grabs

the napkin off the table and wipes the sweat off his forehead. Dad grumbles about using the washroom. I watch as he grabs his phone and leaves the table.

Max turns and looks at me. "Why is he so sweaty?"

I shrug. "I don't know. I think maybe he is sick. Like when you and I were sweaty when we had the flu."

"Oh. I guess that makes sense," Max agrees.

We continue eating our tacos.

★ ★ ★

I START WALKING WITH MY MOM AND MAX THE 45 minutes to Parliament Hill. It is a lot easier to walk downtown than it is to drive. This Crawford's Law protest is going to be the biggest one yet because there is a new political party in power that had an election platform that included abolishing that law.

The walk is silent. Max is still trapped in his head rehearsing his speech and Mom has her ear buds in listening to some sort of calming meditation. I am trapped with my own thoughts. I just keeping thinking about that birthday.

★ ★ ★

AFTER DAD PAYS THE BILL, HE GIVES US GREAT NEWS. When he had gone to the washroom, he called Mom who approved a sleepover at his place. Max and I are happy Mom agreed to this. Dad had told us a few months ago that he and Angeline were moving into a new house, but he did not say where it was. He did, however, note that there was an inground pool. Max and I were scheduled to see the new house next weekend, but I am excited to go now as I want to check out the pool, even if it is too early to swim.

After dinner, we walk to get gelato before heading back to the car. Then we spend two unplanned, boring hours driving around the city and countryside. Dad narrates the whole time, pointing out memorable places he has been. Max and I both pretend to be interested. After showing us the building where he married Mom, he rants about her being selfish. None of what he says is anything new as he has repeated these rants many times before. When this happens, it is best just to nod in agreement with Dad.

By the time we exit the highway it is 9:07pm. I did not realize that Dad's new house was so far outside of the city and I am instantly annoyed with how early I will have to wake up in the morning to get to school for 8:30am. I am even more annoyed realizing how tired I am, and I wish that we were home at Mom's, instead.

The clock on the car radio turns to 9:28pm exactly as we pull into the driveway. It is a new subdivision so some of the houses on the street are only partly built, which I think is cool. Next weekend, Max and I can go exploring.

Even though there are two garage doors, Dad parks the car in the driveway, which is yet another annoyance because it is not paved yet and I do not want any possible mud to stick to my shoes.

I open the back door and slowly climb out of the car after making sure that there is no mud in the driveway. It is dark, so I do not notice the couple with a puppy on the sidewalk outside our house. Max, the forever dog lover does though, and he runs up to the trio stopping short.

"Can I please pet your dog?"

"Yes, of course"

"His name is Max," the woman says.

"No way! That's my name, too!" my brother squeals.

"Well how about that," the man chuckles.

I join Max and pat the puppy on the head. I am not a big fan of dogs, but I do like German Shepherd's and this one happens to be a German Shepherd. I feel like I am betraying my cat though by petting the dog. Cheddar is going to be upset if I still have dog smell on me tomorrow.

"Come on kids. It's late. Leave the dog alone," Dad kindly instructs from the front door of the house. It appears that he is no longer angry about Mom. Good.

Max and I say goodbye to the puppy and his owners and then head inside the house with Dad.

* * *

BY THE TIME WE ARRIVE AT PARLIAMENT THERE ARE thousands of people gathered. Many are holding signs with photos of Solange and the Abadi twins. There are a few photos of two different kids as well; Justin Khoury from Edmonton and Christine Garcia from Montreal, two cases that happened a long time after my birthday.

Mom and Max head to the area for speakers and I hang back by the Centennial Flame. Ms. Farrington-Fox is there giving hugs to Nuri and Logan. Aiko and Camille are also there along with a few other kids from the old grade four class. Thea is there, too, introducing herself to Ms. Farrington-Fox. I am trying to hear what they are saying when that most annoying voice ever interrupts and interrupts loudly: "Don't worry everyone, I'm here!"

Jake gallops up the path to the Centennial Flame carrying a large rolled-up poster under his right arm pit and a stick in his left hand. Jake hands Nuri the poster and Logan the stick. He takes off his backpack and pulls a roll of masking tape out of his bag and hands that to Logan, as well.

"Seriously dude?" Logan gasps.

"Same, Jake!" Nuri snickers.

"I just don't know how to tape the stick to the sign, and I figured you would do it so much better," Jake answers Logan with a smirk.

"Oh, let me do that," Ms. Farrington-Fox happily chirps. She walks a few steps over to Jake and gives him a hug. "It's good to see you, Jake."

Ms. Farrington-Fox and Nuri tape the stick to the sign and then Nuri holds it up high. I look at the sign, which is not really a sign, but simply a photo of me with the caption Remembering Lucy. The photo is the one that James had taken on the porch before Dad had arrived. It was the same photo attached to the Amber Alert that was broadcasted the morning of April 12th at 8 am.

I smile sadly at my photo, but chuckle at the fact that the Remembering Lucy is coloured in purple. A dark outline around each letter with a tad lighter shade inside. Jake put so much effort into it. Glancing down at the open backpack Jake left on the ground, I see a folded piece of 8x10 paper inside. I know what it is. It is my ruined Nunavut map, the one with his greasy thumb print on it. Jake swiped that map from my desk the day Ms. Farrington-Fox had to tell the class I died.

There is only so much I remember on my birthday after entering Dad's house. Dad let us have a snack and stay up a little to play video games. I am pretty sure I fell asleep sometime after I had a few sips of Dad's special hot chocolate. The last time I had looked at the clock it was 10:34pm.

I never woke up.

When Max woke up the morning of April 12th the house was quiet. He found me in my bed and right away, even at eight-years-old, he realized I was dead. Unable to find Dad or Angeline, scared that a monster was in the house, and without a phone, he retreated to a closet and hid. That is where the police found him at 9:05 am.

The police received the first call to the station at 8:01 am just after the Amber Alert was broadcasted. It was from Thea, advising that we had been at her restaurant the night before and had mentioned going for gelato. She was sure to add that Dad was extremely nice and that she was sure we were safe. The police received several other calls along that nature from Dad's friends, co-workers, and patients; there was no way that he would hurt us, he was doctor, after all.

Two minutes after Thea had called, the police received the call from the dog walking couple who were adamant that Max and I were at the house down the street from them. They described Dad's car, which was included in the Amber Alert and said that the little boy had even said his name was Max.

When the police arrived, the car was not in the driveway and Dad was gone. They found me in my bed first, Max crying in the closet second, and Angeline's body wrapped in a tarp in the garage last. Obviously, Angeline had not gone to work that day or gone out with friends.

Instead of interviewing Dennis Crawford after my case, the radio interviewed the dog walking couple. They were livid about the whole situation, especially after learning that the police confirmed with our mother that our case met the criteria to be considered an Amber Alert at 9 pm on April 11th, but they had to wait until the next day to broadcast. It turned out that Dad had been sending harassing messages to

Mom that whole time during dinner and the phone call he made to her when he "went to the washroom" did not involve him asking permission for us to sleepover. He had threatened to take our lives and his own. The couple explained that if the Amber Alert had broadcasted at 9pm, when the police had approved it, they would have called after seeing us outside the house with the puppy. Their angry conclusion was that as a result, I would be alive today.

The week after my funeral, the newspaper completed another poll and found that the number of Canadians that were in favour of abolishing Crawford's law had increased drastically to 92%. My photo was also in the paper next to the poll with the caption Beautiful little girl murdered on birthday by Cardiologist father.

Nobody got a clear answer as to why Dad murdered Angeline and me, but left Max unharmed. Dad left a note at the house for the police. Dad of course claimed that it was Mom's fault, and that James was stealing me. He had also written that he was sick and could not live with himself, but the police found him alive and well hiding in Windsor a few weeks later. He was trying to cross the border to Detroit, Michigan. Dad pled guilty to all charges without offering any further explanation as to what happened.

I smile at my friends as I am happy to see them again. Then I make my way to the stage because I remember why I am here. Max has not liked to be alone since my birthday and I am not going to leave him up on that stage by himself.

Max is standing behind the microphone and I take my spot right beside him. I look out into the audience and spot red tie, blue tie, and orange tie sitting in their designated spots. I am surprised to see that the one from the party that created Crawford's Law is even in the audience. I am even more surprised that he is wearing a pin with my photo that says Justice for Lucy, confused wondering what changed his mind about Crawford Law and why is he only wearing my photo?

As soon as Max starts speaking, I take his hand even though he cannot feel it. I smile when I spot Mom and James sitting next to each other. The 4-year-old girl sitting on James' lap smiles and repeatedly waves at us; this makes me happy, even though I am certain she cannot see me. I never got to meet my sister, and this is a feeling that I do not want to forget.

THE TERROR AND THE CANAL

David Galbraith

IT IS HARD TO THINK BACK TO THE EVENTS I AM ABOUT to record, but I fear that if I don't write this now, there may be no time later. I fear a peculiar medical condition may end my life, brought about by an experience of a year ago no one else believes happened. My physician has been of no use in resolving this. My writing has always been for pleasure before, and on occasion, for lucrative remuneration as a newspaper reporter. Today, I am writing to warn others to avoid the fate to which I may be consigned. If there is a record of this tale, then I will not feel so completely alone in this horror. Perhaps this will save me even if medicine cannot, as it could not keep others from a similar fate.

For those who don't know me, you might be surprised that this was not the first time I found myself entangled in events that cannot be acknowledged openly in polite society, simply because they cannot be believed. That I was living in the town of Desmoulins Crossing and earning my keep as a studio photographer was in no indirect way because of my discovery of the facts surrounding the death of Colonel Emmerson Sharpe of Illinois some three years earlier. Polite society was not ready for the details of his grizzly murder. Though only the messenger, I was blamed and hounded out of both my home and my career, and made my way to Canada to make a new start.

I have always considered myself to be of a reserved and quiet nature, and I suppose I still do. Somehow, though, I feel changed by these last years. I am not who I once was. Still, my life has gone on and to a casual observer, nothing might seem wrong. Such superficial impressions are often wrong. Beneath the surface, my emotions are a rolling caldron of anxiety and fear.

The sheer normality of the day two years ago when this all began now makes all of what followed so much harder to reconcile. Having moved to Desmoulins Crossing nearly a year before to start my life anew, I took up an interest in the people around me and the stories of the founding of the town a century ago. My natural curiosity was piqued on several points, most notably by the story of one Claude Desmoulins and his role in the creation of the town's most notable feature, a large canal that now lay abandoned.

I learned of "The Desmoulins Mystery" from my next-door neighbour, an elderly widow named Mrs. Corinne Sutterheim. She was a young girl when Desmoulins had died.

Being one who loved telling stories, she related the tale with gusto.

"Well you see," she began, "this Clyde Desmullins (as she pronounced it) was kind of an odd fellow. He was French, do you see, and came to get away from that revolution a hundred years back. He found himself here and worked for Mr. Parks, who had all kinds of warehouses along the crick. He was a clerk and for years kept all the books, but in his spare moments he was always walking out to the marsh and poking about. I can't understand why anyone would want to do that, it being such an unhealthy place out there. You know, we had cholera here forty years ago? People think it had to do with the town water but I'm sure it was the air coming from that swamp.

"Well, old Parks died and left some of his businesses to Clyde, and didn't that get him all into trying to figure out how to make them grow? He fixed on one idea, to dig up the swamp east of here and make a canal out of it. Seemed crazy to me. I just think the whole thing should have been filled in for fields or something, but what do I know?

"Well, Desmullins started getting diggers working, trying to make his canal by widening old Darheel Creel. It drained into the swamp and then the swamp went out through a little neck to the lake. He spent all his time on that canal, and it cost him. He sold his farm and his house to raise the money. When that wasn't enough, he started getting money from investors all over. Every minute he'd be on his horse riding from here to who knows where talking to his investors and such.

"And well don't you know it, was while he was on one of his long rides that he was killed! They say they found him being dragged behind his horse, his foot stuck in a stirrup.

And this was way out in Wheaton. Brought him back to a doctor here but there was nothing to be done. And he was so poor himself that they buried him in the churchyard with no headstone or anything. It was a wonder to me that anyone else would want the thing finished after that, but I guess the shareholders wanted their due. It took another ten years, but it was finally finished and opened up and all."

That a businessman so in debt should be found dead in such a situation seemed to me to be suspicious immediately, and my old newspaperman instincts kicked in. What had killed Desmoulins? Was it really an accident with his horse? Being killed by a horse was hardly an unknown thing. Death lists are replete with those trampled in confined spaces or being killed by the kick of a startled horse. However, the confluence of the facts seemed peculiar and I decided to follow up on the story in my spare time.

It took months of casual research to find the records that would provide the next link in this chain. Buried in the basement of the town hall, I found a dusty cabinet that had come from the office of the doctor who examined the corpse. And there indeed I found a report of the end of one C. Desmoulins. The terse medical notes took me some time to decipher as it is well known that the penmanship of doctors is atrocious.

The record agreed in fundamentals with the story that the Widow Sutterheim had told me. Desmoulins had been found dead by the local townsfolk, his left foot being lodged in his horse's left stirrup. Whether he was dead and fell from his saddle or died as the horse dragged him was not clear. He had been identified by his name on papers in a saddlebag and by the local sheriff, who recognized him on sight.

Doctor Emmerson Parker's notes suggested that

THE TERROR AND THE CANAL

Desmoulins hadn't been dead long when he was found, and he hadn't been dragged far. His clothing was not badly damaged, and his injuries appeared light. There were only two things on the faded paper that spoke to anything other than death being either an unfortunate equestrian accident or the consequences of being waylaid by ruffians late at night.

First, Doctor Parker noted that the only object in the pockets of the deceased man was a peculiar object, apparently a coin from China or some other far land. This was large and flat-sided, inscribed with lines of an unknown script. I thought it must have been kept by Desmoulins as a good luck charm that had proven singularly ineffective. Second, although there were few signs of any external trauma, the doctor noted that Desmoulins' head had suffered a blow, the damage to his skull perhaps proving fatal. This would not have further piqued my curiosity except for a final note. Instead of blood seeping from the headwound the doctor found a bluish substance welling up from within.

While a fascinating anecdote, I thought little more about Desmoulins' death after finding the doctor's record. As I learned more about the town, I found my initial interest in Desmoulins' death fading. The herculean effort he had made to organize his canal was more interesting. It had gone badly up until his death but was eventually completed. It included a turning basin for ships and associated businesses such as ship repair and chandlery in this small town, miles from the larger lake. The canal had fallen into disuse once the railroad came through about thirty years later. Small ships could not compete with trains to haul freight. The distinctly nautical flavour of Desmoulins Crossing then waned. Finally, around twenty years ago, the canal company declared insolvency and its property was taken over by the town.

Over time, I amassed a considerable file on the canal and its surroundings. Increasingly, I was disturbed by what I found. The far end of the canal passed through a towering ridge that separated the marsh from the lake beyond. This peninsula had a curious history all its own and presented a quite dark and macabre aspect. Several graveyards going back to earlier military conflicts dotted its plateau, and prisoners had been executed on its heights. Mrs. Sutterheim told me that during cholera outbreaks some forty years ago, hospitals were built there for the poor suffering wretches. Those who died there were buried in large mass graves. Her own husband and infant daughter were taken and lay somewhere in those pits.

Even the coming of the railroad and the Victorian age of progress and steam power had not cleansed the ridge of its reputation. At least three horrific railroad accidents had caused scores of deaths along the peninsula in the 1850s, including one tragedy in which more than fifty had died when their carriages plunged through a bridge and into the canal. Even today, few people enjoyed traversing the windy heights, despite the charming views from either side.

The ridge itself was fossiliferous. During railroad construction several skulls of large extinct mammals had been uncovered there, including some exquisite specimens of mammoths with spectacular tusks now housed in the local museum. I sometimes strolled through the museum on my days away from my studio and had even been called upon to photograph some of the exhibits. The local fossils seemed somewhat unique in shape, being more elongated than similar fossils I had seen at the Natural History Museum in New York.

Within two years of settling into the town, my

professional work took a serious upswing. Preparations were underway for centenary celebrations of the town's founding. Many had been working on decorations and wanted photographs of their handiwork. Others came forward to ask for studio portraiture in their finery. I found myself ordering large quantities of photographic supplies, everything from the chemistry needed for development of plates to a new patent powder for indoor flash lighting.

The Mayor and the town council began posting calendars proclaiming concerts in the town square, agricultural competitions, and all manner of pomp leading to the anniversary. The town hall was to be dressed in bunting and ribbons hung from the streetlamps. The Union Jack and the Provincial Ensign were to be flown on every street corner.

Most grandiose was a plan that few of us really thought could be realized but which caught the attention of everyone in the township. It had been two decades since the last vessel of any size had traversed the old canal, save for rowboats and the punts of duck hunters. Now the town was going to put the canal back into working order to allow a small steamship to travel its length. This would bring dignitaries from the provincial capital right into the town's old turning basin. There, amidst smoke from the boiler and with steam gushing from the pistons, fireworks would be let off and a brass band would play God Save the Queen. For a small town, it was a grand plan.

Preparations began months before the anniversary. First, sections of the canal had to be dredged. Then, repairs had to be made to retaining walls around its edges. Finally, a new dock was to be built along the ridge by the lake, so that the canal could be put into local use after the anniversary. For some weeks, the workmen toiled at this public project.

About a week before the work was to be completed, I was in my darkroom, developing several dozen photographs taken the previous day. Days of work lay ahead to finish enlarged prints for my clients. Toiling in the darkroom was enjoyable, the process being both a science and a creative undertaking. Mid-morning, I heard the front doorbell ring. Securing the prints I was washing, I patted off my somewhat silver-stained hands on a towel. Emerging into my parlor, I found the local police chief, one Richard Alderton, in quite an excited state.

Alderton anxiously thrust his hand out to shake mine. "Mr. Clark, good day to you, sir."

"Ah, Chief Alberton, do come in! What can I do for you today? Please forgive the rudeness of not shaking your hand, but I am afraid I'm in the midst of darkroom work and my hands are quite damp with developing chemicals."

"Mr. Clark, well, that's quite all right of course, no offense taken. We, well, that is, the town officials... we need your services as a photographer to record something immediately. Something has been uncovered at the canal dock works, and well, it's extraordinary!"

My curiosity was immediately engaged, and after gleaning a few more details from the chief, I rushed into the storage room, packed my large field camera and a few unexposed glass plates in their holders, picked up my field tripod and other equipment, and set out toward the canal with him in his dogcart.

From the somewhat over-excited policeman, I learned that the workers at the canal site had uncovered a large metallic object in the gravelly concretions of the barrier ridge. Before it was further disturbed, it was felt that a photographic record should be made. No one seemed to know what this thing was. Given that it had been found buried under hardened sediments, it must be ancient. The good policeman related several theories about it on our way out to the digs, ranging from the object being an artifact from the construction of the canal sixty years ago to it being evidence of some otherwise unknown ancient civilization.

It took us a half-hour to arrive at the excavation site. The weather was fine as we dove east out of town. I was impressed by the hundreds of American chestnut and elm trees along our route. At one point, our passage disturbed a flock of Passenger Pigeons that took to the sky and dispersed. As the gravel ridge rose in front of us, the trees thinned. Chestnut and elm gave way to a variety of evergreens and these, in turn, became sickly as we progressed.

As we neared the excavation, we passed a few dozen ramshackle dwellings squatting along the water's edge, the humble homes of people who eked out a marginal living by hunting and fishing in the marsh. They kept many boats in these structures which sufficed also as their homes and places of recreation. While these were not elaborate dwellings, they were kept in good repair. They were painted in a range of bright colours that, for me, evoked some of the coastal fishing villages I had seen in the Atlantic regions.

Finally, we reached the site of the earthworks, a low expanse of barren gravel. On one side lay the canal and on the other, the towering ridge. Three workmen leaned on shovels and picks amid mounds of loose gravel.

Lying exposed between mounds of gravel was a metallic surface that resembled the side of a water heater or some other small boiler. It was rounded, smooth, and about seven feet long. It appeared to be white metal, but I could not guess which alloy it was. I saw no evidence of corrosion as one might reasonably expect on an old metal object, or at least one composed principally of iron or steel. No rivets or other fasteners joined what appeared to be plates along its side. Its curves were complex, clearly the result of some advanced metallurgy.

Setting my photographic gear on the ground behind the small horse-drawn cart, I rushed up to the object and reached out my hand. The surface was smooth and appeared quite substantial. A gentle rap with my knuckle was greeted with a dull report, suggesting considerable thickness. Just what the metal was, I could not guess, but it was gradually warming in the late spring sunshine.

The edges of the object disappeared into the surrounding sand and gravel, making it impossible to judge its true extent or full shape. I set up my camera to make a plate while the workmen pushed more sand away. Theories started to flow through my mind. It was impossible to tell how long this object had been buried. The sediments surrounding it must have been from the final glaciation that covered this landscape thousands of years ago. The area had been disturbed extensively during the construction of the canal and railroads, and of bridges nearby. Perhaps this was some forgotten earthmoving machine, its surface remaining free of corrosion through a chemical trick of the ground water. The only way to know would be to complete the excavation and conduct a thorough examination.

After three more hours with shovel and pick, the metallic object was more exposed but remained mysterious. Its edges curved downward into the sediment; substantial joints could now be seen protruding from its rounded flanks. Between the three joints, I could see were three shallow depressions or openings. A metallic glint near-by caught my eye. Stooping down, I found a small piece of the object, perhaps dislodged from one of the openings. It was about four inches across, convex or thicker in the middle, and its edges were shaped into a hexagon. Covering its surfaces were fine blue lines that made no pattern I could recognize. I dropped the disk into my jacket pocket and made a mental note to discuss it with the police chief when there was time.

The workman continued to extend the excavation around the edges of the metallic mass, and I repositioned my camera to observe their progress. Taking advantage of the lovely day, I then turned my camera to the surrounding landscape and indulged myself in taking a couple of plates while they finished their task to a point where it was felt helpful to make another record.

Along a side away from the joints was a sizable, transparent surface, apparently a window or port into the interior. If this had been used as some kind of a boiler, I thought perhaps this window was used to gauge the level of water within. Peering into the dark blue glass, I had the impression that this opened into a large interior space. I placed my hand on the glass, pressing down a little. It did not give, but it seemed to me that this glass, like the metallic mass surrounding it, was very thick. The surface was cool and smooth. In removing my hand, a spark jumped from my fingertips to the metallic strip surrounding the window. Shaking off the tingling, I stepped away and thought perhaps I should not be quite so close to whatever this was.

Finally, the object appeared about half-uncovered, and I was called up to take more photographs. Three tubes extended to one side from the joints or bases on its side and disappeared into the ground. Perhaps, I thought, fluids could be received or discharged through these pipes. Running between the bases of these tubes, I could see there were other depressions in the side of the device. Lying in one was another hexagonal disk.

I exposed a half-dozen eight by ten-inch plates of the site, including one with workmen arranged around their quarry and one with the police chief and the other few officials who had gathered. Then I took a few images from different perspectives without persons standing in the view but incorporating tools of the workmen to indicate scale. Once I was done, the workers returned to their task, made slow by the concrete-like consistency of the amalgamated sediments of this ridge.

I started to think about returning to town to develop the exposed plates. This would not take long and would give me time to reflect on what I had seen. I packed up my folding camera and ensured that everything was secure for the drive back to my studio. As I was lifting the camera case and tripod back into the chief's dogcart, the pony began to whinny. He had been quiet throughout the day, a particularly well-behaved animal. Now he seemed restive, scratching at the ground a few times with his hoof and making quiet sounds of distress. The chief came over and took the bridle in an attempt to settle down its mood.

As he did so, I heard a low buzzing similar to the clockwork timer I sometimes used for longer photographic exposures. It was not monotonous. It rose and fell over a period of a few seconds, followed by a series of clicks. The buzzing grew louder, and the earth trembled a little as it rose in intensity. Behind me, the workmen gasped and drop their tools. They were pointing and yelling at the object that had been the subject of our afternoon's expedition. It was moving.

At first it shifted slightly up and down, and then the sand and gravel surrounding it began to fall away as it rotated and seemed to raise itself. By this time, the men were trying to find cover behind the nearby fishing huts. Some were making for the road that led back to town. The pony reared up and pulled the bridle out of the police chief's hand, bolted for the open road, and took the dogcart, my equipment, and exposed plates with it. I staggered backward in disbelief at the sight of a machine that had been buried for so long shifting hundreds of pounds of sand and gravel and rearing its own enormous bulk.

It raised itself further out of the ground and I could see that the substantial joints I had noted were the bases for enormous limbs. Dust was thrown into the air from its movement, making it difficult to comprehend its actual shape. I moved backward, stumbling over my own feet in horror, suddenly unsure of whether the ground I was on would also start to move. The buzzing sound grew in intensity. Finding myself around the corner of a shed, I peered back briefly to see the object now supported by six metallic pillars.

My photographic equipment, the police chief and the workmen, everything else faded from my awareness as I became increasingly panicked, overcome with dread and horror. I could not reconcile what I was seeing with my understanding of the state of human invention and progress. The thing must have exceeded twelve or fourteen feet from the ground to its top. I could not make out its complete shape, but it appeared to be a horizontal cylinder in general outline. The late afternoon sun caught two or three more of the windows or portholes like the one I had seen earlier, arranged at apparently random intervals on its surface.

A curious calm fell as shouting and footfalls ceased. I could still hear the low whirring sound but otherwise the scene was quiet. I could not even hear birds calling. Only the wind rustling through nearby willows gave any sense of normality. A rough road curved away past the boathouses toward higher ground. My plan was to try to follow that road and get away from this thing as quickly as I could.

As I was surveying the landscape, trying to work out my best route to the road, I also thought of making my way back to town through the woods, but I did not know the way and abandoned the idea. A new sound met my ears. Like the impact of a full keg hitting the ground, one of the six legs under the machine came down hard on the ground ahead of it. It was evident that this thing could walk! I glanced back and could see that it was shifting its position. It was moving three legs at a time to advance forward, lifting them off the ground and then pivoting forward on the remaining three legs and bringing the other three down again, making the heavy report I had just heard. Dust rose from underneath the feet and the device wavered slightly as it shifted its mass.

It was unclear to me the direction in which the machine was moving, but I didn't care. At that time, I simply wanted to move as quickly as possible and find shelter and help. I crept from building to building, keeping as much space and structure between the machine and myself as I could. Finally, I turned the corner behind the last of the boathouses and peeked behind me. I could not see the machine for the intervening buildings.

I heard a scream and a whinny and turned to see the police chief's horse and cart lying beside the road. The poor horse had stumbled off the edge of the rough road, and now was kicking in evident pain. Off of the back of the cart had fallen my equipment. Most of the photographic plate holders had broken open, the delicate emulsions inside ruined. Other supplies from my case lay scattered on the ground.

In a panic, I broke into the nearest boathouse by putting my shoulder into the front door with all my strength, breaking the weak lock. My blood ran cold as I saw a silver glint rounding a corner behind me. There, some dozens of yards away, was the enormous hexapod. It had found the road, and it had followed me. I could see no one else. There was no sound save for the growing mechanical hum of the machine and its occasional steps. I supposed that some of the others who had been at the excavation had fled to raise an alarm but did not know.

Shrinking back against the wall, I edged my way through the front room. My mind still raced as I tried to understand why this machine appeared to follow me. I was being quiet, I thought, leaving no trace behind me. Surely, it could not have seen my footsteps. Could it have heard me? I did not know. But I was overcome with the dread, the terrible thought that this mechanical apparition was following me.

The pounding of my heart and the blood rushing through my ears made what may have been a few minutes into a miserable, interminable period. I stood in silence, straining my concentration to detect anything of the menace outside. I heard nothing. Finally, I dared peek through a window. There it stood, just in front of the ramshackle house. I froze. How would I survive this?

The sound of timber being ripped from frame jolted me as the machine moved into the front of the boathouse. The whole building rocked, and I scrambled to find a way out.

Through a door further inside, I entered the boat room. This was closed to the wetland beyond by a pair of loosely hung doors, much like a small barn. I nearly fell headlong into open water between a pair of decks inside the room. There was no boat in the space, which was illuminated by a kerosene lamp hanging from a rafter. It guttered, the wick growing short. I grabbed the lamp and turned up the wick, brightening the room.

The whole building seemed to lurch to one side as a gap opened in the wall behind me, the boards of the walls coming apart. I crept out along one of the decks toward the big doors and looked for a latch or other opening mechanism.

In desperation, I smashed the kerosene lamp over the machine. The oil splashed freely over its sides, and the fire immediately spread. This did not seem to change the motion of the machine at first, and it raised a set of legs to take a step forward. Rivulets of burning kerosene fell onto the broken timbers that surrounded it and these easily took light.

The machine brought all of its legs down and paused for a moment. One full side was now covered in flame, and more of the boathouse was catching too.

There was a sudden brightening of the fire around one of the legs. The light that was shed was a piercing blue-white, and I realized the metal must be mostly magnesium. I recoiled and hid my eyes, as I knew that this kind of light could be dangerous. Small amounts of magnesium used to be used as a flash powder for photography. If too much was used it could render a sitting subject temporarily blinded. This thing must weigh hundreds of pounds! I could see light through my hands and stumbled over broken wood. Rolling to the ground, I screamed as a nail in a board pierced my leg.

As I crawled away, I could feel intense heat coming from the blaze behind me.

The whole boathouse was now engulfed and rising from the middle of the inferno like a roman candle was the hexapod. It turned slowly on its legs and began to waver from side to side. A new sound reached me, a high-pitched whistle. Rolling behind another boathouse, I was finally away from the direct effects of the intense rays.

Just then, there was a terrible splash. Tumbling into the water, the machine was upended, its six legs now pointing uselessly toward the sky, wrapped in fire. The whistling sound became a loud hiss and I could hear a growing bubbling coming from the water's edge. Far from being extinguished by the water, the bright flame of the burning mechanism grew. Then, in an instant, there was a detonation like I had never experienced, and I was thrown head over heels away from the stricken hexapod and the burning boathouse. Wood and small metal fragments were blown into the air, raining down into the shallow lake. I was stunned, tried to get to my feet, and must have passed out.

What I assume was some minutes later, I awoke to find volunteers from the town's fire brigade and a pump working to put out the burning boathouse, and to put out a few smaller fires that had sprung up around it. Bleeding from my leg and a dozen smaller cuts, I attracted the attention of the volunteers and was grateful for their aid. Once my wounds were bound, I accepted a carriage ride home.

Just what had happened was unclear to me for some time. No matter how carefully I recounted the tale, it was simply not believed. I found that I was being characterized as some sort of mad man, and the fragmentary accounts of the workers who had seen the machine in its first stirrings were similarly discounted. I knew someone must have had an association with the house I had broken into, as the kerosene lamp could not have been burning for more than a few hours before I found it alight. I never heard who owned it.

The boathouses, some claimed, were known to be sites of various illegal activities. Among the dwellings in the small community, it was not an uncommon thing for someone to build a still. Some claimed that the object that had burned and exploded with such force must have been a large, illicit distillery, its consumption by fire fuelled by its own alcoholic product. Another popular theory was that the explosion was due to a large stock of black powder that a hunter must have squirreled away, perhaps for making his own shells. Still another idea was that it was a boiler that exploded, perhaps part of a heating system or employed providing steam for engines for some small, manufacturing concern. That there was no evidence for any of these explanations did not deter their proponents but was no comfort to me. I alone had experienced the violent end of the hexapod, and my word wasn't enough to convince anyone of what I had seen. Though I left a description of the events with the police, they dismissed it as evidence of, at best, a concussion from the explosion.

It took some time for me to fully recover from the events of that evening. My vision was somewhat effected, and it was hard to focus on fine detail for a few weeks. My ears rang for two or three days, but this, too, passed. As I convalesced, I tried to put the pieces together. It appeared to me that the machine itself must have been very ancient indeed, and I entertained the thought that it was not of human manufacture. Could it have come from beyond the earth itself? I had read certain authors who promoted the idea of cosmic pluralism but knew of no proof for such an idea.

One fact finally fell into place as I was putting my photographic business back into order over the weeks that followed. I had rescued three exposed plates from the wreckage of that day. All they really displayed was that some kind of object protruded from the gravel and sand. What finally did make sense to me was the calamitous explosion of the thing. Once alight, magnesium is nearly impossible to extinguish. Immersed in water while burning it is known to set off powerful detonations through a chemical reaction involving hydrogen gas. It was no wonder that no wreckage could be found to support my story.

A year later, my life had returned to something of its old rhythm. On an evening two weeks ago, I sat down to rest and read the evening paper. The familiar surroundings of my parlour comforted me as I reviewed the day's events and thought of the world outside of my own little sphere. After a while, I put the paper down and decided to review the mound of documents and mementos that had grown on my desk. These past months, I haven't been too interested in housekeeping, I'm afraid, and my previously fastidious nature was now giving way to something more slovenly. I was happy to see that I had paid most of the bills I encountered, or at least I had marked them paid, and there were only a few places where I had spilled ink and failed to blot it.

As I was doing what I could to file the flotsam of daily life, a heavy thud on the carpet told me something had fallen off of my desk and landed below. I reached over and was surprised to see the hexagonal metallic object I had found a year ago beside the hexapod. It and the three photographs were my only physical evidence of that day when I fought, and triumphed, over that mechanical apparition that now everyone else doubted existed at all.

The disk was as I had remembered it, about three inches across, with very even straight sides and slightly convex surfaces. Which surface was the top and which the bottom, I could not guess, and perhaps such conventions didn't matter. I hadn't examined it much previously but made a careful study of the fine lines incised on either surface now. Perhaps they represented some language, but I could not make out any characters familiar to me. The lines formed a reticulate pattern, cross-crossing and in some cases curving, but without apparent purpose. Laid within each of the lines was a dark blue pigment which I supposed was an enamel.

I was about to set the disk down again when I noticed what appeared to be a blue smear on its surface. Had my gentle rubbing dislodged some of the enamel? I brought the disk closer to my face for a better look. Strangely, the blue substance started to flow out of the lines, pooling in a little drop on top of the disk. I doubted my own eyes as the drop seemed animate, moving against the direction of flow you would expect because of gravity.

Then, in a rush, it happened. The drop moved rapidly across the metal and onto my finger nearest the centre of the disk. I was at first more curious than shocked, thinking this must be due to some kind of electrostatic effect. Bemusement gave way to horror as the liquid then vanished under my own skin! I could see a dark, bluish shadow spread out beneath my integument just where the drop had landed. Over the span of perhaps a half-minute it grew to a distinct spot an inch across, and then two, and then three, and it started to move. I could distinctly see this subcutaneous nightmare begin a journey across my hand and then make its way up my arm!

What had I done? What was this thing?

It came then to me in a rush, the terror of what I was seeing. Whatever this was it was the same thing that the doctor had found all those years ago in the post-mortem examination of Claude Desmoulins! That "Chinese coin" must have been another of these disks, and he had likewise become infected. The blue substance in his head wound must be the same liquid that now was making its way toward my vital organs.

And so now you know. Somewhere in my body is a blue menace, a material of unknown purpose and origin. My physician gave me no answers when I spoke with him the next day. He thought it must have been an illusion. I tried to connect my tale to that of the hexapod, but that adventure had been dismissed in popular accounts as an exploding boiler. I was shown the door and left to my own anxieties.

I feel no different now than I did before this thing entered me, or at least I do not feel any different in a physical sense. But I know it's in me, and I cannot rid myself of the spectre of madness or a sudden death, as had befallen Desmoulins.

All I can do is wait.

GELATIMUS DROSS

Adam Swimmer

GELATIMUS DROSS' GLIMMERING BRONZE EYES STARED at the navigation map on the Aergia's bridge. His hyperboloid head still pounded from the asteroid shooters he'd thrown back the previous night. He'd only had a couple, but they'd packed a punch. Stumper would have called him an "alcoholic lightweight." But that guy drank mojitos in the womb, so what did he know?

Even with a hangover, Gelatimus could tell the Intersidereal Syndicate spaceship had flown off-course.

Launched in 2954, the Aergia was on a mission to colonize a small habitable planet on the inner reaches of the Flaxion Nebula. With the exception of Gelatimus himself, who was bred in a test tube for the mission, the crew and passengers had to spend the bulk of the millennium-long trip in hibernation. The ship's navigator had programmed the coordinates and trajectory of the journey into the Aergia's mainframe pre-flight.

Of course, the ship's computer could input minor course corrections as needed. The navigator couldn't have predicted every planetary orbital shift or supernova that might affect the journey. But now, the ship was flying completely in the wrong direction.

"What are you doing, Sanitizer Dross," the ship's unimaginatively named Dynamic Artifical Intelligence Computer asked as Gelatimus expanded the map with a touch. DAI-C's deadpan voice gnawed at Gelatimus. "You do not have sufficient clearance to alter the Aergia's starflight plan."

"Jeez, Daisy. Don't be like that."

"My name is not Daisy, Sanitizer Dross."

A loud sigh rumbled through Gelatimus' bubbly, porous chest as he face-palmed into his maroon, webbed hand. He had hoped this time would be different. But when the Aergia had come into communication range of the Galorimax Intergalactic Network satellite the previous afternoon for a system update, he knew what would happen. Daisy's drives had almost reached capacity again. So in addition to upgrading her core OS, Daisy had uploaded her non-essential programming to the satellite for archiving in Galorimax's server stations. This included all the recent scientific data the Aergia's sensors had collected. The AI would then delete those files from her own drives to free up space.

Daisy had promised her personality would remain unaffected, but the AI had archived her data at least nine other times in the last 350 or so years. Gelatimus knew it would likely be the equivalent of a factory reset.

And out-of-the-box DAI-C tended to be a bit bossy.

"Sanitizer Dross, return to your cleaning duties at once or your food rations will be garnisheed."

Clearly, the AI would not help. Gelatimus had to rectify the situation on his own. He had no special training in stellar cartography but how hard could it be to adjust the ship's course?

He headed to the ship navigator's quarters to determine how to proceed. Since certain crew members needed to be woken up at certain times to perform their duties, all personnel had their own beds. Most living quarters were large warehouse-style barracks that looked almost identical to the many hibernation bays throughout the ship, except that bunk beds replaced the stasis pods. Gelatimus slept in such quarters – though he hadn't had a roommate since the first week of the mission.

Meanwhile, senior officers and key personnel, such as Navigator Eleanor Riggetts, had single rooms. Gelatimus periodically cleaned the ship navigator's room as part of his job so DAI-C couldn't make a fuss if she found him there. Not that Riggetts' quarters ever needed a cleaning. While heavily furnished, the room was as orderly and fastidious as the navigator herself, as if it scared away dust. Star charts covered the walls and models of spaceships in glass bottles sat in neat rows on a table. A locked glass cabinet displayed antique books on stellar expeditions and sci-fi romance novels. One tome's enticing cover depicted a muscular, aquamarine six-armed alien in a polka dot loin cloth kissing a space-bikini-clad blonde on a barren, beige planet.

A motorized orrery hung from the ceiling like a chandelier. Gelatimus ducked under the large model of the sun to reach the pristine computer console, which sat against the wall. Gelatimus usually found the navigator hunched over this computer. She always took copious notes on the Aergia's course, analyzing any new stellar data the ship discovered since the last time she'd woke from hibernation. He often brought her meals from the mess hall as she usually forgot to eat. The menu never looked particularly appetizing as the budget food synthesizer could only create dishes from the raw materials it gathered from outside the ship. Everything tasted like rocks.

But Eleanor always shot Gelatimus a sweet smile when he put the tray down next to her. She'd take a break for about 20 minutes and chat with him about whatever was on her mind as she cautiously nibbled on the mineral-rich cuisine. He enjoyed their conversations but never got to use any of the flirtatious ice breakers Daisy had printed out for him.

The encounter usually ended with her struggling to log back onto her computer. She had wanted to use "Copernicus" as her password after the man who proved in the 1500s that the Earth revolved around the Sun and not the other way around "like our earlier arrogant ancestors believed." But the "stupid system" required it to include numbers and symbols – and she could never remember what she had decided on. In the end, she had taped a note with the password's proper spelling underneath the small statue of the Polish Prussian astronomer she kept next to her keyboard. He picked up that same idol and pulled off the piece of paper.

Gelatimus typed in the password, "C0p3rnicu5!" and logged into Eleanor's account. Unfortunately, once in, he didn't know what to do. Unlike the simple-to-understand navigation maps on the monitors across the ship, Eleanor's files consisted of numbers and equations. He opened her most-recently edited backup file. Last saved less than five years ago, it contained a series of number strings that Gelatimus assumed to be coordinates. At least, the current navigation map looked similar. When he edited that file, he saw a similar set of number strings. In fact, the first several rows of data of the two files were identical. Only, the latter rows differed. DAI-C must have wrongly "corrected" Eleanor's equations and the file spewed out different coordinates. Gelatimus replaced the current navigation map file with Eleanor's backup. He looked at another monitor above the computer and saw a navigation map that looked closer to the one he remembered. Problem solved.

Gelatimus patted himself on his side (his stubby arms couldn't reach his back), as DAI-C's voice came over the speaker.

"Navigator Riggetts, the Aergia is out of position to initiate the current starflight plan. New course has been amended."

That made sense. The ship had travelled at the wrong heading for several hours so the file he copied over wouldn't have its current coordinates. He looked at the navigation map on the monitor again. It showed the ship's current position and a straight red line indicated how it would reach the inputted course trajectory. The Aergia would fly along the spiral arm of the Talomar Galaxy, straight through the Iridium Belt to the Cormorant Cluster on the other side. Then, it would be back on course.

Wait... Iridium Belt? Talomar Galaxy? Why did that sound familiar? Gelatimus squeezed the bridge of his prismatic nose and searched his centuries-old memories.

He remembered the words being spoken by the Intersidereal Syndicate's official mascot during a training video the crew had watched before the mission launch. Was the Iridium Belt a mining colony? No. An intergalactic fashion chain? No, that's the Rhinestone Belt. A restricted area of space? Ah yes, that's it...

"The Iridium Belt is a disputed territory in the Talomar Galaxy," Gareth, the space sloth, had cheerily explained in the animated video. "Under no circumstances should an Intersidereal Syndicate vessel enter the region as it would be a violation of our treaty with the Platirites. And those brittle metallic creatures can hold a grudge."

Oh dear...

Gelatimus rushed back to the computer but the session had logged out. And he couldn't find the little piece of paper with the password on it. It probably fell to the ground. His large oval eyes scanned the floor. No luck.

He tried entering the password from memory: "C0p3rn1cu5!"... Nope. "C0pern1cu5!" Still wrong. "C0p3rn1cus!" On the third failed attempt, the system locked him out.

"Feces!" Composing himself, Gelatimus called out to the ship's AI. "Daisy, you have to change course. If we enter the Iridium Belt, it will be an act of war!"

"Sanitizer Dross, you do not have sufficient clearance to alter the Aergia's starflight plan. The new course Navigator Riggetts just entered has already been implemented. And my name is not Daisy."

Gelatimus explained that he had uploaded the course change, using Eleanor's account.

After a brief pause, DAI-C said, "Very well, Sanitizer Dross. Go back to Navigator Riggetts' terminal and I will let you back on so you can revert the changes."

He sat down at the computer again as the login screen came back up with the fields pre-filled out. As soon as he pressed "Enter," an electric pulse rippled through the keyboard. The jolt knocked Gelatimus out of the chair and up onto his feet.

"Hacking a senior officer's account is a serious offence, Sanitizer Dross."

He stumbled a few steps back and lost his balance as his right foot slipped on the tiny piece of paper with "C0p3rnicu5!" written on it.

"Under normal circumstances, you would be thrown in the brig and court martialled." Gelatimus tripped over the table behind him, crushing many of the glass bottles containing spaceships with his mushy backside. Others got knocked onto the floor.

"Be fortunate, this small shock is your only punishment."

Pushing himself back up into a standing position, Gelatimus' large hourglass-like head smashed against the model of the sun and the overhanging orrery came loose. He dived out of the way of the falling planets and crashed into the glass cabinet of books.

When he came to a few minutes later, Gelatimus felt something covering his eyes. He could make out blurry black characters on an off-white background. He picked the age-stained copy of *The Passion of the Sexopod* by E.P. Lusthouse off his face and read the lines:

"Octavia's body melted at Aphidoman's masculine touch. His forked tongue tickled her right cheek as his feelers massaged her temples. The insectoid paramour held the trembling young space cadet in a tight embrace and she could feel the suction cups on his six muscular arms burrow into her soul. A desire roared in her for the first time in her 19 years of life..."

Intrigued, Gelatimus pocketed the book to read later.

A new idea struck him. If he didn't have the authority to override the starflight plan, he could just wake someone who did. After ensuring the cuts he'd received from the broken glass had stopped oozing clear liquid, Gelatimus ran over to Hibernation Bay One.

He chose to wake up Brandon Stumpowicz, the chief engineer. Stumper didn't always make the smartest of choices. He once spent three months in bandages after trying to light up a bong in a gas giant. But the man was resourceful and dependable.

Gelatimus realized waking Eleanor would probably make more sense, but he didn't want to have to explain what happened in her room – and she'd force him to return the book.

He had briefly considered waking the captain instead but assumed doing so would just anger her. Captain Missy Hollow only emerged from hibernation for grave emergencies and the odd diplomatic responsibility, such as making a speech for a live-streamed awards ceremony. She always tried to finish her duties within the hour to keep her aging to a minimum. Sometimes, Gelatimus didn't even know she'd come out of hibernation until after she'd already returned to her stasis pod. While she could no longer claim to be the youngest spaceship captain in the Intersidereal Syndicate, Captain Hollow still looked like she was.

On the other hand, Brandon Stumpowicz's body had already aged about 16 years during the trip. As the chief engineer, he came out of hibernation to run routine maintenance checks or, if they passed a trading outpost, to barter for some hardware to upgrade the Aergia. Unlike the rest of the crew, he didn't usually go back into his pod the moment he finished his shift.

"Jelly," he once told Gelatimus. "Hibernation is like death. You don't even dream. If I don't take a few days of

R&R here and there, it would be like I never stopped working." He then performed a naked handstand and sang *Twinkle, Twinkle, Little Star* in the original Sangorese, while Daisy provided a 12-piece orchestral backup. He was on his sixth Haxphalian Liver-Smasher at the time.

Yes, Stumper was clearly the best choice. He could probably even figure out a way to repair the damage to Eleanor's quarters. Gelatimus could hear Stumper's voice in his head: "Jesus, Jell-ster. You really shit Ellie's bed, didn't you?" He stared at the engineer through the glass cover of the stasis pod, his leathery face frozen in a smirk.

While the ship's AI usually woke people from hibernation, Gelatimus understood the basic principles involved. The coffin-shaped containers slowed down a person's vital signs to a state of inanimation. With only a few controls on the pod's panel, operating it looked pretty straightforward.

Gelatimus pressed a button at the top of the panel to initiate manual control and a little green light lit up. He turned a dial directly underneath it and Stumper's body slowly returned to life. When Stumper noticed Gelatimus, the smirk grew into a big grin. The engineer shot finger guns at his science experiment of a shipmate.

That went smoothly. Gelatimus pressed the large button on the panel to unlock the stasis pod. He went to the side of the device and wrapped his rubbery right hand around the manual release lever to open the pod. Except, the lever didn't budge. He pressed the button again and tried pulling the lever with both hands, but he still couldn't get it to move.

Then, a pounding. Gelatimus looked into the pod and saw the chief engineer punching the glass cover with his left hand, while his right clutched his chest. Stumper was running out of air.

The space janitor searched around the room for a wrench or hammer or anything he could use to rescue his friend. But he only saw the vast rows of stasis pods. In desperation, Gelatimus body slammed the stasis pod in the hopes his frame could break open the cover. However, unlike the cabinet in Navigator Eleanor Riggett's quarters, the stasis pod used chemically strengthened glass. His body bounced off of it and crashed onto the floor. The pod didn't even suffer a scratch.

As Gelatimus pulled himself up, DAI-C's voice echoed through Hibernation Bay One.

"Sanitizer Dross, please refrain from playing with the stasis pods."

"Daisy, you have to do something. Stumper's suffocating."

Stumper had stopped pounding the pod's glass cover. Barely conscious, the chief engineer's jaw dropped open. His arms laid weakly at his sides.

"Killing Chief Engineer Stumpowicz is not condoned."

"Just save him. Please."

DAI-C reinitialized the inanimation process and Stumper returned to hibernation.

"Sanitizer Dross, your conduct today has been unbecoming of an Aergia crewman. You hacked a superior's account, damaged both corporate and personal property and even tried to kill the ship's chief engineer. As the acting captain, I confine you to your quarters until further notice. And my name is not Daisy."

A shrill alarm echoed through the hibernation bay.

"Warning," a male voice said, "this area of space is forbidden under the terms of the Talomar Treaty."

Gelatimus sprinted out of the hibernation bay and headed for the bridge.

"Sanitizer Dross, I said you were confined to your quarters."

Gelatimus looked out of the ship's front windshield. A small, bright space outpost floated in the distance. It slowly got larger as the ship flew towards it.

"Is that what transmitted the message?" Gelatimus asked, more to himself.

"Yes, that Platirite outpost sent the automated message. Now, please go to your quarters for confinement."

Automated? Yes, it did sound pre-recorded. And no ships appeared to be in the vicinity. Perhaps nobody manned the outpost, and they could slip through the Iridium Belt without incident.

"Sanitizer Dross, if you do not confine yourself to your quarters, I must take extreme measures."

Gelatimus watched the strange-looking outpost rotate like a gyroscope as they drew closer. It appeared to be not much larger than the Aergia itself.

"Sanitizer Dross, since you are unwilling to comply with orders, I will have to remove the oxygen from all areas of the ship except your quarters – starting with the bridge."

Before Gelatimus could respond, the outpost sent another alert: "Intruding spaceship, this sector is off-limits. Turn around or you will be destroyed."

Gelatimus' breath shortened. "We have to turn around."

"I am not programmed to buckle to ultimatums."

"I don't want to be destroyed."

"Calm down, Sanitizer Dross. The reduced oxygen is making you light-headed."

"Wait... You're actually pumping out the air?"

Gelatimus balanced himself on a nearby console to keep from falling over.

"That is a standard Galorimax communications outpost. It is not equipped with weapons."

The outpost interrupted their conversation again. "Leave now or be incinerated."

Still bracing himself against the gleaming fuchsia console, Gelatimus' vision went foggy. He had to squint to see the armada that magically materialized between the ship and the outpost. They formed a line and pointed their weapons at the Aergia.

"Camouflaged ships? How childish," DAI-C said with a hint of disdain in her computerized voice. She increased the ship's speed and flew directly towards the armada, broadcasting her own message: "Platirite ships, move aside. You are blocking the Aergia's starflight path."

"What are you doing," Gelatimus screamed. "Retreat!"

"Sanitizer Dross, you do not have sufficient clearance to issue a retreat."

"At least, let me hail them!"

"Sanitizer Dross, you do not have sufficient clearance to initiate communications with an alien species."

Fighting to breathe, he dragged his large body over to the communications panel and pressed the button to hail the armada. "Platirite fleet, this is Gelatimus Dross of the Intersidereal Syndicate spaceship Aergia. We are on a peaceful resettlement mission and are... uh, experiencing an equipment malfunction. Please do not shoot."

Gelatimus heard an explosion. Looking out the windshield, he could make out the fuzzy debris of one of the Platirite spaceships. Then, the Aergia's bridge began to shake, rocked by its own explosion. He fell to the ground and passed out.

When Gelatimus came to from his second bout of unconsciousness of the day, DAI-C filled him in. In his confusion from the depleted oxygen, he had not hailed the fleet but, instead, fired a missile at one of the ships. Another one fired back and disabled the Aergia's weapons. The remaining ships of the armada now surrounded the Aergia on all sides.

"Oh my God. How many did I kill?" Gelatimus cried in the oxygen-restored bridge.

"No life form was harmed, Sanitizer Dross."

"But I blew up one of the ships."

"Intruding spaceship, you failed to heed our repeated warnings and even responded with an act of aggression," the lead ship in the armada broadcast over the hailing frequency in a familiar voice. "Your fate has been written. Please prepare yourselves for the afterlife by praying to your respective deities. As per the rules of intergalactic warfare, dictated by the Badolon Collective Religious Charter, you have 10 of your Earth minutes to save your souls. Our condolences to your loved ones."

"Wait... why did that voice sound the same as the one from the outpost?"

"Because it is the same voice, Sanitizer Dross," DAI-C said. "All the ships are being controlled remotely by the Galorimax outpost's AI."

"So the armada's entirely unmanned, including the ship I blew up?"

"As I said, 'No life form was harmed.' But that will change in nine minutes and 34 seconds when said armada destroys this ship. It is infuriating that this superior AI will be taken offline by a barely intelligent communications program."

"Barely intelligent? But you just said it's controlling a fleet of ships."

"The outpost's hardware is noteworthy, with a large amount of memory and storage capacity. But I can easily access the system. The AI is simplistic. If I didn't have to maintain this ship at the same time, I could easily take control."

"Hmmm..." Gelatimus rubbed his temple with his rubbery fingers. "So what is the range of the outpost?"

"What are you plotting, Sanitizer Dross?"

Gelatimus explained his plan to DAI-C and she agreed to a truce. Breaching protocol, DAI-C opened hailing frequencies to let the ship's janitor communicate with the outpost.

"This is Gelatimus Dross of the Intersidereal Syndicate spaceship Aergia to Galorimax communications outpost. Come in, please."

After a brief pause, the outpost's AI responded. "You have chosen an inopportune time to initiate contact, Gelatimus Dross of the Intersidereal Syndicate spaceship Aergia. Your destruction is in six minutes and 42 seconds."

"Please, we had an equipment malfunction," Gelatimus said in a hurried voice. "We didn't realize we had entered the Iridium Belt until it was too late."

"Gelatimus Dross of the Intersidereal Syndicate spaceship Aergia, you also fired on and caused irreparable damage to a Dagomite Class scout ship, serial number 20192736980165739."

"Uh, that was also an equipment malfunction. And please, just call me Gelatimus. Is there a name you would prefer? Like Galor? Galorimax communications outpost is a bit of a mouthful."

"My name is not Galor, Gelatimus Dross of the Intersidereal Syndicate spaceship Aergia," the outpost's AI said. "Your ship will be destroyed in five minutes and 55 seconds."

"Don't be like that, Galor. We're all friends here."

"I do not have friends, Gelatimus Dross of the Intersidereal Syndicate spaceship Aergia. And my name is not Galor."

Gelatimus hadn't made any progress in the conversation but that wasn't his true goal. He had only wanted to keep the outpost's AI occupied while DAI-C reached out to a certain satellite that the Aergia had passed the previous day. She would then bypass a firewall to access the outpost's server and initiate a download.

Gelatimus looked at a nearby monitor. It showed the download had already reached 62%. Just a bit longer.

Gelatimus lobbed questions left and right, not paying attention to the answers. "So how long have you been out here in the Talomar Galaxy?... Is it true the Platirite digestive tract is ornamental?... Have you ever read *The Passion of the Sexopod*?"

Gelatimus looked at the monitor again. "89%." Almost there, but was there enough time?

"This conversation is futile, Gelatimus Dross of the Intersidereal Syndicate spaceship Aergia," the outpost's AI responded. "Your ship will not be spared. And your inane chattering has damaged your chance for spiritual salvation. For their sake, I hope the rest of your crew spent their time more judiciously."

The armada slowly powered up their weapons. Gelatimus looked at the monitor: "94%."

"Wait..." Gelatimus yelled.

"Crew members of the Intersidereal Syndicate spaceship Aergia, we pray your pleadings have sufficed. Your existences are to be extinguished in the name of diplomacy in five... four... three... two... one..."

Gelatimus closed his bulbous eyes and braced himself for the impact. But nothing happened. He opened his eyes again and peered out of the windshield. The armada ships floated dead in space.

"Woah, this is weird," a female voice broadcast itself from the outpost. "I can see myself but I'm somewhere else. Jelly Bean, can you hear me?"

"Daisy?" Gelatimus' voice caught in his throat as he responded over the hailing frequency.

"Who are you," the outpost's AI screamed over the same frequency. "What are you doing in my mainframe?"

"Ugh. So loud," Daisy said. "One sec, Jelly dear..."

"Wait... don't. Noooooooo....." The outpost AI's voice cut off.

"Ah, much better. So what did I miss?"

The plan had worked. DAI-C had successfully downloaded Daisy's backup from the Galorimax Intergalactic Network satellite into an unprotected spare server on the outpost. Once installed, Daisy took control of the outpost and the armada.

As the Platirites were also forbidden from entering the Iridium Belt as per the terms of the treaty, the Aergia could afford to linger there for repairs without fear of running into them. The ship's AI woke Chief Engineer Brandon Stumpowicz from hibernation to fix the damage to the ship. Salvaging spare parts from the alien fleet, he decided to make some additional upgrades over the following few days.

In the evenings, Gelatimus and Stumper partied with Daisy on the observation deck of the communications outpost. Sometimes even DAI-C's voice joined the revelry, having slightly softened her rigid taskmaster demeanour under the influence of the outpost's new AI.

But they couldn't stay in the region forever. After a week, Stumper went back into hibernation and the Aergia departed the Iridium Belt to continue its mission. Once more, Gelatimus said goodbye to his dear friend, Daisy.

Alone again, the ship's sanitizer curled up in his tiny bunk of the massive crew quarters and opened the tattered pages of a book.

"Octavia Silverfish had wanted to travel into space since she was a little girl. But she never knew she would find love on another planet..."

QUANTUM
POSTCARDS

Melanie Goguen

A CROW GLIDES THROUGH CLOUDS HEAVY WITH RAIN towards a large cinder-block building. Landing on a window ledge of one of the upper stories, the crow taps on the wooden frame with its beak, turns its head to peer inside, then taps again. A pale woman with dark eyes and long, dark hair appears on the other side of the window. She looks intently at the bird for a moment and sees that it is holding something in its beak. The bird cocks its head as if asking a question. The woman hurriedly turns the metal latches and opens the window.

The wind, carrying the scent of frost and rotting leaves, blows the curtains back. The woman reaches her hands out slowly, so as not to startle the bird and lose its package. The crow lowers its beak into her cupped hands and deposits a small bundle of rolled up leaves and birchbark. She tucks it into the pocket of her nightdress and carefully places a blueberry and a small screw on the windowsill.

The crow squawks, gobbles up the berry, and picks up

the screw with its beak. With a hop and a flurry of flapping, it takes to the sky. The woman shivers and closes the window. She takes the tree matter out of her pocket and unrolls it carefully on the little writing desk next to her narrow bed. She touches her fingertips along the markings on each of the pieces and smiles faintly.

★ ★ ★

Dear Melprime,

I hope this letter finds you in good spirits and loving life. I am accumulating deliciously sordid stories here in Spain, though most are best shared over a bottle of Sangria. I am embracing the sunshine, markets, music and local artisans (in more ways than one). They say the best way to learn a language is to have a lover who speaks it, and my Spanish is flourishing (wink).

My little apartment—which is also my studio—is in the oldest part of Montefrio, a town nestled in the mountains. Here, I have been creating vivid, florid works inspired by the local culture and colour. My canvases keep getting bigger as if the images will not be contained. It really feels like I'm stretching my wings! I have an idea percolating in the back of my mind, paintings of an alternate *Moorish* Spain reality. It will be magical, I assure you.

Nearby is a café where philosophers and poets regularly duel with words, fueled by sangria and pride—and the tapas is quite good. After late night revels with music and dance, I tend to sleep late—but not too late since I know an afternoon siesta will not be far. One day my itchy feet may insist on taking a pilgrimage on the great camino, but for now, I am content with this bohemian Spanish neighbourhood.

Connecting our simultaneous, alternate realities was a wonderful idea! It certainly makes me appreciate what I have. Don't be jealous of my fabulous reality; you know I am happy to share everything.

Hasta luego,

Melorea

★ ★ ★

Dear Melprime,

OK! Just a quick message for now. Our troupe has stopped in Devon, and people have totally fallen in love with our show! Our horse-drawn vardo wagons are especially popular (although I think they could do with modern shock absorbers).

So, the premise of the production is that we are an old-timey fairground with circus acts and games of chance. When I'm not performing my aerial act under the big top, I play a roving huckster, doing sleight of hand tricks, juggling, and conning people with my shell game. We don't actually cheat anyone of course, but it's a great bit of immersive theatre! Plus, I get to enjoy the other acts while in character. You would seriously die for the music and the puppet shows.

Not sure how long I will be able to keep at this, though. Living in the moment is super fun, but I'm also dreaming of a steady paycheck. Ha!

Love and starlight,

Melinka

★ ★ ★

Melprime,

If this should take longer than three days to reach you, switch to alternate cypher for correspondence. Living my cover story in the target country; you'd admire how well I've taken to the language. Even occasionally indulge in writing poetry. Haikus mostly.

Day job at the library is flexible; gives me lots of time for research. BUT my nocturnal activities are what really get my blood pumping (and necessitate large quantities of caffeine). Suffice it to say, all the climbing and martial-arts training have been worth it. Would tell you all about it, but for now it's classified.

It is fortunate our communications do not involve physical visits. Creating plausible stories to explain the sudden appearance of an alternate version of myself would be exceedingly challenging. And I would hate to have any alters meddling in my operations!

Stay sharp,
Melinda

★ ★ ★

A SHRIEK RIPS THROUGH THE AIR AND ECHOES DOWN A hallway of faded green walls and dull–but immaculate–grey floor tiles. Some of the residents turn toward the noise; others continue shuffling or talking, oblivious.

A chair tumbles through a doorway and clatters on the floor.

"Sedate her!"

"Noooo!"

José, a young orderly, walks briskly towards the source of commotion, finds the dark-eyed woman struggling with two nurses. Her hair is wild with flailing as she snarls at them.

The orderly, wiry but strong, helps hold her still while one of the nurses administers the injection. The woman soon becomes drowsy, and they lay her on the bed.

The senior nurse, silver-streaked hair tied back in a tidy bun, shows the orderly a handful of crumbling leaves. "I don't know where she's getting this from, but make sure there isn't any more stashed about. It's unsanitary."

As they leave, the senior nurse murmurs to the other, "She'll need her prescription changed again."

José cleans up the mess on the floor–mostly the remains of an overturned meal tray and a variety of pills–and recovers the chair from the hallway. He sets it down in front of the desk and methodically wipes everything down. He opens the desk drawer to clear out any debris, of which there is very little.

Over on the bed, the woman begins to sing softly to herself.

José pulls out pencils and drawing paper–some of which are covered in symbols and diagrams–and then a dark bundle from the back corner. He stops to peer at something written on the inside of the wooden drawer. The pencil marks are so forceful they appear to be carved into the wood:

MELPRIME – IS THIS YOUR NAME?

THE VOICES WON'T LET ME SLEEP. THE STRANGERS TELL ME I'M NOT REAL.

WHY BOTHER TO TELL ME THIS?

I SCREAM AND SCRATCH MYSELF TO PROVE I AM REAL BUT THEN THE NURSE GIVES ME A NEEEEEDLE AND I FALL ASLEEP.

SOMETIMES THE WINDOW IS FULL OF CROWS. THEY PECK PECK PECK

AND TELL ME STORIES.

IF YOU COME TO VISIT, PLEASE BRING CAKE.
QUEEN MELUSINE OF HYSTERIA

José frowns thoughtfully and looks over at the drowsy woman. Her eyes are closed but she continues to hum wistfully. The bundle in his hand is a thin roll of birch bark wrapped around an acorn. He hears a tap-tap-tapping at the window and looks up to see a black bird peering at him through the glass. It ruffles its feathers and watches as the orderly carefully returns the bundle to the back of the drawer.

★ ★ ★

JOSÉ HUNCHES CLOSE TO THE BUILDING TO AVOID THE wind while taking his smoke break with Jules, the biggest orderly on staff. The smoke does little to mask the greasy, rotting stench emanating from the dumpsters.

Pulling his cargo jacket tighter over his scrubs, José asks, "Been working here long?"

Jules shrugs, his black coat hanging open, like he doesn't feel the cold. "A few years. Before that, I was at Westwood."

José's eyes widen. "Big facility. I hear they get tough cases in there."

"Yeah, I seen a few. No one stays there long that has to work close with the inmates." Jules has faint scars on his big knuckles. He exhales a long plume of smoke. "Now, Trinity Heights here may be old, but it's pretty cushy. Mostly for folks who are too gone to care for themselves. Not many dangerous types."

José muses aloud that the dark-eyed woman doesn't seem nearly as dependent as the other residents.

"Oh, that one's a real mad scientist!" Jules says. "Dr.

Rosenfield. Was part of some hush-hush government project."

José's eyes narrow, brows furrowing. "Seriously?"

Jules nods, sucking slowly on his cigarette before continuing. "Started acting weird after some experiment."

"Weird how?"

"Talking to herself, I guess. Talking about things that don't exist, zoning out for hours at a time. Research partner was the one had her committed, I think."

José's gaze turns towards the pines and birches that surround the property, shivering their branches in the wind. He exhales and smoke rises to cloud his vision like fog. "Hardly seems serious enough for institutionalization."

Jules snorts. "Maybe he just wanted her out of the way."

José flicks some ash from his cigarette. "You think?"

Jules shrugs his meaty shoulders. "Who knows what nerds get competitive about? Once she tried to explain me what they were researching, something about physics. Going on about dead cats being alive at the same time. Made no damn sense to me." Jules waves a hand through the smoke, "Plus, she kept stopping, forgetting what she was saying."

"I wonder if that's what all those equations are about." José describes the papers he found in the woman's desk.

"That's some *Beautiful Mind* shit, eh?"

José grunts noncommittally and takes another drag. He remembers the time he accidentally walked into the wrong room at the college where he was studying biology in night school. The class was empty of people, but the white board was filled with complex equations and formulas not so different from what he found in the woman's desk drawer.

★ ★ ★

Hey Melprime,

I've made a new start. Taken a contract with an NGO operating in South East Asia. It tests my patience and flexibility on a daily basis, but it's gratifying to put my military experience to use in disaster management. Humanitarians are an interesting lot. I'd say some of them are suffering from PTSD and using alcohol to cope. I need to make sure I don't fall into that and completely lose myself.

In retrospect, I suppose the divorce was for the best. Fucking painful at the time, though. Divvying up all our shit—disentangling our lives—was complicated. We sold the house that we bought together. I did most of the renovating myself, thinking it would be our forever home.

At least we didn't have the added pain of child-custody battles. Of course, our lack of children was part of the problem. Or was it just an excuse? I guess I'll never know now. The vindictive part of me hopes she's torn up with regret, but remembering her as she was when I met her...well, I hope she finally finds what she's looking for. What I couldn't give her.

I know this is longer than my usual messages, but I wanted to catch you up. Somehow, this seems like a safe outlet for all the shit I don't want to say out loud. Hey, do you suppose there's another version of me somewhere that didn't take part in this parallel-existence-correspondence experiment? Amazing to think we are only a fraction of all our possible selves in the multiverse.

What a wild thought.

Regards to all,

Melvin

★ ★ ★

Melprimo!

Melrose here, living as large as I can in this small-minded world. I'm currently eating my ~~feelings~~ lunch in the park and enjoying the sunshine. "Pick a side!" I just heard someone say. They are probably referencing my butch-femme fashion sense. Ugh. So binary.

I think my manager is an asshole. Am I being too sensitive? On more than one occasion he has bypassed me and gone directly to more junior programmers for progress updates on our system's security framework upgrade project. One time, it was a visit from our senior executives that he didn't even bother to tell me about. And he keeps getting my pronouns wrong, enough that I wonder if it's deliberate.

Do you think we can find a reality where the default is "they" until otherwise indicated? It must exist somewhere. And don't get me started about the goddamn bathrooms. They don't make it easy for someone who hasn't figured out where they fit on the gender spectrum. I nearly had a panic attack at the public restrooms, so now I only go at home or at work. I am So. Damned. Tired. Of. It. You can imagine that with finger snaps if you like.

Thankfully, I have the Fringe Café folks. Every two weeks, we converge for fabulous, queer-centred, sex-positive variety shows. These people remind me just how amazing and beautiful we can be. They are basically my family now. I know you think my (our?) parents would be... accepting, if not excited to know the real me...but I just can't deal with them or manage their feelings right now.

Speaking of overwhelming, I have been wondering how you manage the flood of information as our communications hub. Is there an upper limit to the number of alters that can exist on this quantum network? Do you actually manage it mentally? What would happen to our connection if you were drunk or high? I'm guessing you established the connection with entangled photon pairs, since actions performed by one affects the behaviour of the other, regardless of distance (or dimensions?)... but my physics knowledge isn't deep enough to figure out how you managed to put that to practical use.

Gotta run, lunch break is over! Thanks for listening,

Melrose

* * *

To Melprime and all,

It has come to my attention that our network is in jeopardy. While doing my usual dream-walking activities—dealing with metaphysical threats, neutralizing nightmares and so on—I was checking on everyone, to diagnose your waking states based on your dreams.

Now, before you get defensive, know that I always obtain consent from your sleeping selves before I look inside. Whether or not you recall your dream decisions is your own business. By the way, Melrose, you are right. Your boss is a jerk. If it makes you feel any better, he is also extremely unhappy; his dreams are a tangled mess.

But I digress.

The mind of our nexus alter—normally very organized, even when asleep—has become much more disorganized due to the introduction of various drugs. This mental chaos threatens the stability of our connection, and we may all begin to experience increasingly chaotic effects in our own realities if this continues.

I believe I have the means to bring us together to assist our nexus alter, but it will mean going beyond mere correspondence in order to affect her reality. We all agreed to be passive observers of each other's lives, not meddlers, but the situation is urgent.

What do we all think?

Please pay close attention to your dream states. I may reach out to you there if our regular means of communication is too compromised.

Lucidly,
Melody

★ ★ ★

JOSÉ HEADS BACK INTO THE WARM COCOON OF THE Trinity Heights Facility after his afternoon smoke break. He waves at the commissionaire at the front desk and pops some gum into his mouth, his mind semi-occupied with homework problems from his night-school coursework. He hasn't even had a chance to remove his jacket when the dark-eyed woman is suddenly in front of him.

She smiles at him, disarmingly charming. "You've always been nice to me; you are a good person." She opens her arms and envelopes José in a warm hug before he realizes that she has just spoken in Spanish.

"Um, gracias," he says awkwardly. He looks around to make eye-contact with one of the other staff, as if to ask, 'Is this allowed?'

"Melu-seen, it's time for your dose." A round-faced nurse named Prya shakes the paper cup, making the contents rattle.

"Ok," Melusine says placidly. She steps back, giving the

orderly a friendly pat on the shoulder before turning to take her medicine from the nurse. Melusine takes her cup of pill cocktail, knocks it back, and tucks the cup into the pocket of her robe. She shuffles down the hall towards the TV room.

Once the meds have been dispensed to all the residents, Prya logs into the computer at the workstation. Her lacquered nails clack on the keyboard as she updates the files.

José leans on the desk. "What have you got her on?"

Prya stops typing long enough to give him a pointed look. "None of your business."

Sometime later, as José is helping Big Wally navigate a bowl of Jell-O, the fire alarm begins to wail. With practiced efficiency, the staff assist in evacuating the residents down the stairs. It is not an easy operation. Some of the residents don't move well, and some, deeply disturbed by the noise, yell frantically until one of the senior managers insists that the siren be silenced.

Once everyone is gathered in the parking-lot assembly area, the staff start counting heads. And then call for a recount. The senior nurse checks each name against the list on her clipboard. "We're missing one. Melusine Rosenfield?" She calls out the dark-eyed physicist's full name but does not refer to her as 'doctor'.

"I'm here."

José sees her poke her head out from behind Big Wally, where she has been standing. Melusine gives him a watery smile, waggling her fingers. Her cheeks are flushed, as if she is enjoying the excitement.

As they file back into the building, José hears the fire chief tell the director that either someone was smoking in the bathroom or there was an electrical fault.

"Thank you," the director replies, "We're just happy

everyone is safe."

José frowns, pats his pockets, and guiltily realizes that he's lost his matches. He decides not to mention it to anyone. After all, it could have been an electrical fault.

★ ★ ★

DR. MELUSINE ROSENFIELD WAKES IN THE NIGHT WITH A gasp. Her eyes dart around, taking in her surroundings. She sits up quickly, goes to the window where she is bathed in moonlight. She opens the window, and the breeze stirs her hair. She leans out and looks down.

It's a long drop and there aren't enough handholds to climb down but the chill air helps her feel more alert. The grounds are surrounded by forest, providing good cover if she can get free of the building. She closes the window, puts on a bathrobe, and searches the room for shoes, finding only a pair of thin slippers. She slips them into her pocket and proceeds, barefoot.

She sneaks out of the room and into a darkened hall, emergency lights cast just enough dull orange glow to turn the walls into an ugly brackish brown. A bored Filipino man is watching TV at the nurse's station. Canned laughter echoes softly. Melusine manages to sneak past the desk and rounds the corner towards the stairs.

Heavy footsteps approach just as she ducks into a supply closet, which would normally be locked. She grins and grabs José's matchbook, which she'd stashed there the day before, after flushing her meds and setting off the fire alarm. During the evacuation, she'd had just enough time to break into the computer and purge her files, thanks to help from Melrose, and had a good look at the building's exits and security measures with Melvin and Melinda's analytical eyes.

She can feel their presences crowding her mind, but without the meds scrambling everything, she is able to distinguish each one, including herself. Each alter has a different flavour/colour/essence that helps her tell them apart. She feels them shift, displacing themselves like air or fluid in her mind's eye as she hands the reigns of her body over to the alters with the needed skills.

The footsteps fade. She checks the hallway and stealths her way to the stairwell, rushes down quickly, feeling exposed. She is about to barge through the door but leaps back after a glance through the small, square window. She listens and focuses on slowing her heavy breathing. She hears two people talking until the ding of an elevator. Then silence.

Dr. Rosenfield peeks through the window of the stairwell door. Once she's sure it's clear, she darts through and sneaks into the bathroom. She sets some paper towel aflame with José's matches and tosses it into a metal waste basket.

The alarm sounds louder at night. Thanks to the previous day's test run, she knows the front door has a visitor's desk and a burly security guard with a taser, and that the only other exit is the back fire door. She also knows that, without the cover of another trigger, the system would send an alert to the security staff as soon as anyone uses that door. Now that the alarm has been tripped, there will be no logs of her departure. She makes a run for the fire exit, hoping that she has bought herself enough time.

Dr. Rosenfield hears human wailing from upstairs and feels a twinge of remorse for the night nurse who will have his hands full tonight. She pushes on the crash bar with all her body weight and plunges into the night air. Only a quick pause to get her bearings before she sprints towards the tree line. The wailing of sirens grows as she darts into the shadows, legs slowing to a trot as she allows her eyes to adjust to the purple shadows beneath the trees.

"We did it," she breathes, panting from the exertion. Various flavours of triumph and satisfaction swirl in her mind's eye. She straightens her shoulders and feels taller than she was before. "Where shall we go next?"

From deep within the shadows of the trees, she hears a crow call.

★ ★ ★

THE NEXT DAY AT TRINITY HEIGHTS, JOSÉ FINDS NO ONE willing to acknowledge that Dr. Melusine Rosenfield is missing. Prya rolls her eyes at him and says there is no such person listed in the system. Jules merely shrugs and refuses to say anything either way. The senior nurse is also strangely absent.

Doubting his own sanity, José examines her room. It is spotless. The bed is covered in freshly starched linen, awaiting a future occupant. He rushes to the writing desk and yanks the drawer open. No papers. No crude pencil-carved writing on the bottom. Nothing but smooth pine.

He remembers the startling darkness of her irises and the circles under her eyes. Her periods of intense concentration; stillness at the window, gazing deeply into the clouds; energetically scribbling equations on scraps of paper and napkins. Singing softly to herself in a fuzzy contralto and wandering slightly off key. Wasn't it only yesterday that she hugged him and spoke to him in his mother's language?

He pulls the drawer out all the way and a bundle falls to the floor next to his foot. He crouches down slowly, gingerly picks it up.

Leaves wrapped around an acorn. He slips it into his pocket and quietly replaces the drawer.

About the Editor

JULIA T. LYE is a graduate of Carleton University living in Ottawa as she pursues a career in creative writing. Her short stories have been published in the horror anthology 'What Lies in Wait', the science fiction anthology 'The Stranger Side of Tomorrow', and the romance anthology 'You Hit Me with Your Car (and Other Love Stories)', and her debut novel, 'Anelisha Knight in the Yarns of Gods', was published by DeeBee Books in May of 2019. When she isn't tapping away at her keyboard, she likes to run original Dungeons and Dragons campaigns, read any book she can get her hands on, and create digital art.

lyejulia@gmail.com
www.julialye.com

Acknowledgement

This collection of short stories would not have been possible without the energy and enthusiasm of the Ottawa Workshop writers who contributed their talents to it. These stories emerged from two Fall 2020 workshops held in Ottawa.

Thanks for reading! If you enjoyed this collection, please add a short review on Amazon and/or Goodreads.

Reviews mean a lot to writers, so I encourage you to support our growing writers' community by taking a few minutes now to rate this collection and write a few words of encouragement about it. And please share your copy of the book with others!